Martyn Kendrick

Anatomy
of a
Nightmare

The Failure of Society in Dealing with Child Sexual Abuse

Macmillan of Canada
A Division of Canada Publishing Corporation
Toronto, Ontario, Canada

Copyright© Martyn Kendrick, 1988

Canadian Cataloguing in Publication Data

Kendrick, Martyn, date.
   Anatomy of a nightmare

Bibliography: p.
Includes index.
ISBN 0-7715-9549-2

1. Child molesting – Canada.   2. Child molesting – United
States.   3. Sexually abused children – Psychology.   4. Children as witnesses. I. Title.

HQ71.K46 1988   364.1'5554   C88-093256-2

Designed by Don Fernley

Macmillan of Canada
A Division of Canada Publishing Corporation
Toronto, Ontario, Canada

Printed and bound in Canada by
T. H. Best Printing Company Limited

DEDICATION

I dedicate this book with hope and love to our daughter, Justine, and to Dr. James Anderson, who long ago made many things possible.

ACKNOWLEDGEMENTS

A s with all such projects, an author is only partially responsible for the finished work. John DeRoo, former pub-
lisher of *Hamilton Cue Magazine*, agreed with the importance
of understanding the phenomenon and made it possible for
me to attend the Hamilton trial. Very early in the investigation, Frank Jones of the *Toronto Star* graciously made available
to me substantial research he had undertaken. So too did Max
Allen, CBC broadcast journalist and producer. Dr. Ralph
Underwager also made available to me an unpublished manuscript. His grasp of the issues, his compassion, and his integ-
rity have been a source of inspiration. Without my agent,
Larry Hoffman, this book might never even have been
started. His commentary and encouragement during all
phases of the book's progress have been invaluable. I must
also sincerely thank my editor at Macmillan, Sheldon Fischer,
whose ruthless criticism clarified some dense passages and
helped structure and refine some of the arguments. Copy
editor Riça Night's painstaking line-by-line attention to the
final manuscript rendered the prose more readable. Doug
Beiers, Rosalind Lanza, Herbert Bailey, and others too
numerous to mention have all contributed in their own way
to this work. Lastly, I thank my wife and friend, Lucille Lanza,
for her company, her insightful commentary, and her commitment to a work that was both difficult and time-
consuming.

As for those flaws and errors that remain, I take full responsibility.

Martyn Kendrick
November 1987

CONTENTS

PREFACE: "Out of the Mouths of Babes . . ." *vii*

1. THE HAMILTON TRIAL: Tail End of a Nightmare *1*

2. A LEGAL DILEMMA: The Line Between Fact and Fantasy *30*

3. THE NORTH AMERICAN EXPERIENCE: Path of an Epidemic *63*

4. SATANISM: Salem Revisited *107*

5. SADISM: Sexual Deviance and Psychopathology *130*

6. CHILDHOOD: The Roots of Violence *155*

EPILOGUE *178*

Endnotes *184*

Bibliography *187*

Index *191*

PREFACE:
"Out of the Mouths of Babes . . . "

Two traumatized young Hamilton girls were separated from their mother, her boyfriend, and their father for a two-year period while a court investigated allegations the girls had made to a foster mother involving grotesque sexual abuse, satanic ritual murders, bestiality, and cannibalism.

It was a bizarre and tragic case. Media coverage of the trial, while as extensive as court limitations would allow, did nothing to explain how such charges could appear in a family court, nor did it even touch upon a much larger phenomenon that was occurring across North America. That same astounding sequence of allegations was being uttered by children — many of them, like the Hamilton children, not yet nine years old — in Utah, Alaska, California, Minnesota, Washington, New York, Florida, and Colorado. Nearly every state in the U.S. had its own sordid story to tell, and some had two: each tale involved not just sexual abuse, which would have been problem enough; not even gross sexual abuse; but ritual sex, sacrificial murder, and the mutilation of young children.

The two little girls in the Hamilton case were repeating unnervingly typical stories. In Ontario, Canada, as in the United States, where the stories had begun surfacing with eerie regularity in 1983, they fuelled rumors of satanic cults existing on the fringes of society and preying on our defenceless children. It was, to say the least, a terrifying thought.

Shortly after the two young Hamilton girls made their disclosures, two young boys who had been cared for by the same foster mother came forward and alleged that their mother and other adults were running a human slaughter-house where children were being massacred. That case was still being investigated as this book went to press. A third, involving a mother allegedly ritually chanting while sexually abusing her daughter, came to court in Toronto early in 1987. During the latter part of 1986 other trials or investigations quietly began in northern Ontario, Montreal, and Vancouver. While no charges have been laid — nor custody battles fought, in civil or criminal court — an Alberta police officer believes and has stated publicly that at least five missing children have become the sacrificial victims of a satanic cult practicing its deadly arts in his area.

The consultant to the Vatican on cult trends, Father Frank LeBar of the New York State Diocese, believes that the increasing number of satanic cult members is bound to cause serious problems. "These practices," he says, "are far more widespread than we would like to believe." Despite his alarming claim, no one knows if "these practices" and the context in which they are said to take place are actually true cases of satanic abuse. As in the Hamilton trial, no material evidence has been uncovered that would substantiate the stories being told by the children or surmised by their adult care-takers.

Canadian (and specifically, Ontario) child advocates have been cautioned by their U.S. counterparts to investigate such charges quietly. The public, the American advisers argue, is simply not ready for this kind of disclosure. They should know.

Beginning in the middle of 1984, a bizarre series of trials began making headlines across North America. The *Washington Post*, the *New York Times*, *Time* and *Newsweek* magazines, and a host of television documentaries and radio phone-in shows gave voice to concern over an apparently rising tide of child abuse — and, more specifically, of sex rings involving children in satanic ritual murders. Like a Greek chorus, the press headlines communicated the fear and sense of outrage that seared the collective consciousness of middle Americans. Schools, daycare centers, and other institutions involved in the care of children became the focus of sex-abuse panics.

The pattern was nearly always the same. A suspicious parent, teacher, social worker, or health-care professional would question a child about sexual abuse. Other parents often became involved. Then the social service and law enforcement agencies would launch an investigation. Based on their suspicions, they removed children from their homes, separated them from their parents, and questioned them repeatedly about sexual abuse. Within a short time, the children began speaking of being fondled and forced to take part in ritual sex, murders, and mutilations. Upon investigation, these stories tended to break down. Nothing could be substantiated.

For a long time, these strange happenings south of the border left Canadians untroubled. "America," we would say, as if that explained it. Such things couldn't happen here. We didn't know then that the legend out of which these obscene tales emerged — "a legend based on fact and embroidered by fantasy," as CBC broadcast journalist Max Allen put it — was being passed on to a new generation of Canadian child advocates. We wouldn't know that until the Hamilton children came forward in the early days of 1985 to spin their tragic tale of horror and woe . . . but that came later.

On October 15, 1984, a prosecutor in Scott County, Minnesota, wrapped up a year of emotional testimony with a surprise release of all but one of eighteen accused child molesters. It had been a sensational case, with allegations by boys and girls ranging in age from four to fourteen that their parents and other adults had gathered frequently to sexually molest them. The tiny community of Jordan (population 2,500) had been rent asunder. Kathleen Morris, a zealous prosecutor profiled in *People* magazine that same year as one of the "up-and-comers," allayed the community's concern by stating that a "criminal investigation of great magnitude [was] under way," and that justice would be meted out in due time.

Following the release, there was a three-month hiatus while the FBI, under Hubert H. Humphrey III, carried on an intensive investigation. On February 15, 1985, (just as the Hamilton children began making their disclosures), Humphrey announced that the statements made by the Jordan county children alleging sexual abuse were not credible because the procedures used in the investigation had "exerted undue and coercive influence upon the children." The "criminal investigation of great magnitude" to which Morris had earlier alluded involved further allegations by certain of the children that some among their number had been murdered and mutilated. Also untrue, according to the FBI's investigation. The allegations had surfaced only after months of repeated interviews by the child-abuse investigators.

The FBI's investigation effectively put an end to two hysterical years that had changed the face of this sleepy midwestern American town, a town that one resident mournfully concluded would never be the same again. Nor would Kathleen Morris, the state prosecutor who had staked her reputation on the conviction of the alleged molesters. Unable to believe that it was finally over and that all but one of the suspected molesters — that one being a man who had admitted his guilt immediately after his arrest — were free to pursue their shattered lives, she exclaimed to the press and through it to the nation at large, "I am sick to death of notions like the presumption of innocence."

It had been an alarming trial, not unlike the Salem trials in late seventeenth-century America to which the press initially compared it. But the reality was much closer in time and symbolic significance to contemporary America. Similar trials were happening right next door. During the course of the Jordan trial, two other major cases involving children accusing their care-workers of involving them in ritual sex and murder were taking place, in California and Vermont. In the latter case, 90 state police took custody of 112 children from the homes of the members of a particular church to have them examined for child abuse after one church member reported widespread mistreatment of children within the sect. After months of investigation and repeated interviews by the authorities, the children admitted that they were molested and forced into unspeakable acts. But given the opportunity, they later retracted their stories; the church member who had originally filed the accusations withdrew his charges. He admitted maliciously fabricating the story, as did the children. The California case has seen all but two of the original seven alleged molesters set free, and all of the children who initially spoke of having suffered obscene sexual exploitation have recanted their original stories.

Children fabricating tales about murder, mutilation, and ritual sex? Child advocates zealously assisting them? State police and the FBI called in to make dozens of arrests on what turn out to be unsubstantiated charges? Is it possible? Is it even conceivable?

As 1985 wore on, equally lurid trials would spring up in towns and cities across the U.S. and Canada. Like a plague or the Pied Piper, something was triggering the minds of hundreds of widely separated young children — some as young as three years of age — causing them to utter words best left unsaid, words that would erase what innocence remained in their scarred and weary young lives.

But once spoken, the tales of murder, mutilation, cannibalism, and pedophilia would echo across state, class, and national boundaries and enter into the lives of unsuspecting families and communities as gruesomely as Charles Manson's breed of multiple murderers had entered into the life and times of twentieth-century America. And the most inexplicable aspect of these trials, for all their painful effects and gory attention to detail, is that they were ushered out of the mouths of babes.

That is where this book comes in. Most Canadians were unaware of the horrific trials going on in the U.S. I came across them as a journalist. But as I began to investigate this phenomenon, something else began to appear. Even stranger than the statements these children were making, (things that, if uttered by an adult, would be called hallucinations or signs of schizophrenia), and stranger than the fact that they were being believed, was the fact that in most of the trials, the allegations were eventually found to be groundless, and the accused persons innocent. Yet the fact that most of the cases were thrown out of court didn't seem to affect the credence given similar accusations being made almost simultaneously across the U.S. Stranger still, the same pattern of unnerving, often-false allegations and the hysterical response to them surfaced in Canada, England, and Australia — again, almost simultaneously.

My analysis of this strange phenomenon has led me to an unusual — indeed, a troubling — conclusion, which it is the purpose of this book to elucidate. I suggest, on the one hand, that given the *context* of their statements — our legal, social, and psychiatric systems — the children are mirroring something about the authorities on whom they depend, representing an aspect of ourselves, our goals, and our intentions. For the most part, this mirroring is performed unconsciously by both the children and the adults who help them to engineer or fabricate a tale of sexual abuse. On the other hand, given the *content* of their utterances, I am led to conclude that the strains of evil in our society — the threat of nuclear annihilation, the degradation of our environment, the calling of life itself into question in abortion issues on the one hand and genocidal wars on the other, the increasingly twisted forms of violence erupting in major Western cities — all these unacknowledged evils are being absorbed by our children and, by various mechanisms, transmuted and reflected back onto the adults they are closest to: their parents and care-givers. As a society, we have projected our faults onto this limited class of adults, who are serving as our scapegoats.

In order to understand this nightmare in the courts, I have been compelled — as have all those who have become close to some of the victims of this phenomenon — to investigate unusually evil realms of human thought and endeavor. The children spoke of Satan, ritual sex, and sacrifice; thus, we too must consider something of this dark lore of Western history. At the same time, the children spoke of murder, mutilation, and cannibalism — terrifying themes that bring to mind men like Ted Bundy, Charles Ng, Ian Brady, or Clifford Olson, who represent an increasingly common phenomenon: the severely disturbed violent multiple murderer.

It is not a pretty picture.

This books opens with a documentation of the phenomenon. Chapter 1 studies the Hamilton case, the first major trial of its kind in Canada. Chapter 2 examines several important U.S. cases, representing a wave of such trials that preceded the Hamilton case. Chapter 3 completes the background, explaining how children can become "mediums" in this unsettling fashion, by detailing our changing views of how children's minds work — the paradigms of childhood. An important sidelight to our changed attitudes toward children involves the ways that the laws designed to protect them have, in fact, eroded certain fundamental principles of justice and endangered the legal and civil rights of certain adults.

With Chapter 4 we begin a more careful study of the historical antecedents to this social phenomenon, looking specifically at the witch trials in Europe and New England during the sixteenth and seventeenth centuries, which employed methods of interrogation that led innocent people — primarily women — to confess to having slept with the devil. Chapter 5 carries the investigation further, with an analysis of psychopathic criminality in contemporary society. Chapter 6 completes the picture by relating the various elements, and showing how adult violence turns up again, in an irrevocable cycle, in the lives and minds of each new generation. The Epilogue draws some general conclusions, and perhaps points the way out of this morass.

A study of this nature is profoundly unsettling for various reasons, not the least of which is that it may be misunderstood. I do not, for instance, wish to deny that many cases of child abuse do occur, with tragic, possibly lifelong, effects. Nor would I try to imply that this is the last word on the subject: psychiatry, history, law, and perhaps philosophy and religion still have much to contribute to our understanding of these issues. I have tried, rather, to show how this phenomenon works itself out in the lives of those most closely connected with children, and how it affects their one practical recourse — the legal system — and their human rights. In summary, I hope this investigation will give Canadians pause and generate some serious, careful thought.

1

THE HAMILTON TRIAL:
Tail End of a Nightmare

When they bury the kids in the graveyard holes we have to go down into the hole and get into the box with all the goo in it. We don't like it. It stinks awful. But we have to do it for the big people or we will be just like the little people in the hole.

Mary Potter, 5 years old, April 1985

Was [the children's fantasy] not evidence of brutal trauma to their psyches, just as would bruises and broken bones be evidence of physical abuse to their bodies?

His Honour Judge Thomas Beckett, Hamilton Unified Family Court, trial summation, March 1987

While an entire nation tuned in to Hubert H. Humphrey III's denouncement of prosecutorial methods in a sensational Jordan, Minnesota, child-abuse trial, a young mother in Hamilton, Ontario, was tearfully arranging to leave her two daughters in the care of the local Children's Aid Society (CAS) for what she expected would be a temporary period while she took some time to rebuild her shattered life. Beverly Potter* knew nothing of what was going on in Minnesota or Vermont or California. She was conscious of little

---

* A Hamilton court order prohibits the naming of the children, their therapist, or any member of their family, or the release of any other information that might identify the children. The names of all persons affected by this court order have therefore been changed. All other information remains true and accurate.

1

more than the tiny, desperate hands that clung to her as she told her children what she was about to do. Her younger child was crying and afraid, but Beverly had no alternative. Abandoned by her boyfriend, alone in a new city, desperately afraid that she would harm either herself or her children, she simply had no one else to turn to.[1]

Taken by her social worker to the home of Jane Wyatt, an emergency-care foster mother, Beverly explained as best she could some of the things that the foster mother should look for. She was crying. She told her confused daughters that she would soon return for them. She kissed them both, told them Mommy loved them, and left.

That was the incantation.

Jane Wyatt, a devout Christian woman who had cared for a great many children during her years of service with the Hamilton–Wentworth CAS, was moderately alarmed by the girls' physical appearance and psychological state. But she had seen enough end-of-the-line children to know that a little love and affection would wipe the tears from their bloodshot eyes — for a time, anyway. And if she couldn't cleanse their souls right away, she could at least give them some clean clothes, some hearty food, and a stable environment. Later she would recall for a spellbound court that the children smelled of "urine and semen" and that the younger one, Mary, who suffered a bladder infection, was inordinately afraid of being touched or seen naked. While bathing her, Jane noted a redness around the girl's vagina. She knew the signs of sexual abuse, and these children seemed to her to have been sexually abused. She wrote as much in her daily journal.

That was the evocation — the day that the nightmarish tale was drawn silently into Canada's collective psyche.

Within two weeks, Jane Wyatt informed CAS officials that the children were terrified of their mother and of her boyfriend William Knight, whom they accused of fondling and of sexually assaulting them in other ways. Over the course of the next three months, these two young girls — aged five and seven, respectively — would flesh out their tale with accounts of pedophilia, pornographic film-making, murder, mutilation, and cannibalism; ultimately the net of these lurid allegations even came to include their father, Danny Blake. When the police informed Beverly Potter of the charges her children were making, she became hysterical. She refused to believe that the children were stating such things, but was denied permission to see them at length alone or to discuss the allegations with them. At the time, and throughout the lengthy trial that ensued, all three accused adults denied their guilt with sustained conviction, although each expressed doubts about the potential of the others for the alleged conduct.

The trial was expected to last approximately 10 days. It took nearly two years, consumed approximately 150 court days, heard evidence from 161 witnesses — including 19 psychiatrists, as well as psychologists, physicians, and social workers — listened to over 20 hours of tape-recorded sessions between the children and various interviewers, and viewed approximately 25 hours of videotaped sessions with the children and their psychiatrist. At the end of the trial, the judge had to review over 15,000 pages of transcript and consider the relevance of 142 exhibits (themselves comprising several thousand pages).

During that time, the closed Unified Family Court room, sequestered in Hamilton's provincial court building, was the scene of acrimonious battles among six lawyers; was adjourned so that Potter could give birth to a third child (who was immediately taken from her and put into protective custody by the CAS, with the ultimate aim of permanent Crown wardship and adoption); and saw the police called in to protect the court from Potter's estranged husband — who, according to Beverly Potter, had "threatened to come and blow away the judge and that whole goddamn army of lawyers if

[she] revealed the existence of his satanic friends." But one of
the saddest scenes court observers witnessed was the young
mother's hysterical breakdown on the stand after a gruelling
cross-examination by her estranged husband's lawyer, upon
which she slipped down onto the cold grey courtroom floor,
curled up into a fetal position, and pleaded with her own
lawyer, who had rushed to help her, "Please don't hurt me.
Please, Daddy. Please leave me alone. I can't take any more."
   That was the devil himself.
   She was rushed to St. Joseph's Hospital in Hamilton, where
she remained for one week for treatment and assessment.
Speaking directly about her breakdown in court, she later
stated:

> I have been questioning me as a person, who I am. And
> like, I'm wondering, like, is there a possibility I could be,
> like I don't know who I am, but is there a possibility and I
> want to rule it right out and I want to know if I did, 'cause
> as Beverly Anne Potter, as far as I can remember, I did
> not do anything like that to my kids. But is there a possi-
> bility that I could have? That's what I want to know. . . .
> I'm so confused because a lot of this stuff has opened up
> a lot of things inside me and I have a lot of feelings and if
> I have my kids, like I mean I would, I would again say to
> the CAS, "Please take them, I'm scared." . . . Maybe one of
> my other selves did these things that you and my chil-
> dren have accused me of.

She was referring obliquely to her own history of gross sexual
abuse during childhood and to recent research findings indi-
cating that a significantly high percentage of grossly sexually
abused children develop multiple personalities.
   One can only dimly imagine the effects of the protracted
trial on this fragile woman. The men, while stressed by the
situation, remain employed and anonymous to the public.
Beverly Potter, on the other hand, has had her children
removed from her care by the very people she originally

turned to for help, the CAS; has been testified against by the people she will in future need to turn to for help, the psychiatrists and medical professionals; and gave birth to a third child during the course of the trial, who was immediately taken away from her (that child's father, her co-accused in this trial, subsequently left her and challenged the CAS's attempt to have his child, too, become a Crown ward). She has lost her job and been accused by Welfare officials of falsifying her returns, effectively cutting her off from receiving benefits in the future. Add to all of this the numbing memories that she has been forced to call up from the depths of her bruised mind and expose before the adversarial court, and one can understand her plaintive cries for help and her confused, self-diagnostic "confession."

Forensic psychiatrist Emil Zamora, who assessed Beverly during her hospitalization, later told the court that while it is true that some persons with a history of gross sexual abuse develop multiple personalities, he did not think that this young woman's symptoms warranted such a diagnosis. Dr. Eva Gede, a specialist in multiple-personality disorders, agreed; she suggested instead that Potter suffered a "borderline personality disorder," which left her prone to such breakdowns. But whether or not the mother's diagnostic confession was accurate, it certainly pointed to her deepening quandary over the allegations. Like everyone else involved in this byzantine legal process, she needed to find an explanation that would satisfy not only the court, but herself. How else was she to understand two years of unflattering, nerve-wracking testimony about her inability to mother? If she was innocent, as she claimed, how else was she to explain the wall of disbelief that effectively cut her off from her children forever? Like everyone else, she was looking for somewhere to cast the blame: surely someone or something must have caused her two young children to utter such horrifying thoughts.

The children were not allowed to testify. At one point, His Honour Judge Thomas Beckett, near tears of rage at the defence attorney's persistence in this regard, shouted, "I will not subject these children to further ritual torture." He was referring to the trial itself, but his choice of words would prove profoundly indicative of his disposition toward the charges.

The children's father, Danny Blake, couldn't bring himself to speak about the satanic allegations directly. He called them simply "the other half." He denied both the sexual and satanic charges in his no-nonsense, forthright diction: "That there stuff about those things are bullshit." When asked specifically about the cause of the allegations, he could offer no clear explanation; like others perplexed by the uncertainties of this trial, he cast about for answers and for somewhere to lay the blame.

> Like you can ask me that, but I don't really know. The response as far as I'm concerned towards [his co-accused] if they are guilty, . . . which they got to be in one sense, because no five- and seven-year-old is going to be able to come up with stuff like that at their age unless they have been shown. So, as far as I'm concerned, it seems fair if they are guilty the punishment should come; if they're not, then that's different. . . . It shocked the hell out of me. . . . I told my wife there that if it is true, God help you, 'cause I told her a long time ago that I put the two kids on earth to turn around and raise them up and have a life of their own, not for two screwballs to come along and screw it up. And she said, "Do you think I could do that?" And I told her, "I don't know. You've gone too far. . . . If you did do that, which you shouldn't have, which is the other half, the sexual part, then I don't want to talk to you."

The obviously tragic aspects of this case confound the mind. Two children, aged five and seven respectively, emerging from a chaotic and occasionally violent background, from living conditions that at one point were labelled a "disaster area" by a public health nurse, are voluntarily given over to the CAS by a frail and abused young woman who has herself been scarred by a series of childhood sexual assaults suffered at the hands of her stepfather, uncle, and other men when she was between four and sixteen years of age. Her own mother had been aware of the assaults, but did nothing to help her — often, indeed, beating her and defending the men who assaulted her. To the mental-health professionals around her, Beverly Potter represented a classic example of the victim becoming the villain, the abused becoming the abuser, unconsciously acting out her own brutal history of childhood sexual trauma on her innocent children.

Prevailing doctrines held by women's groups, child psychologists, and child-protection workers maintain that speaking about unspeakable things that happened to one in one's childhood at the hands of one's parents or other adults is the best therapy against the low self-esteem, depression, and other disturbed mental symptoms that can develop as a consequence of childhood abuses.

According to this view, many of those who do not undergo some form of therapy — or at least find an empathetic and supportive figure to talk to — are prone to repeat the abuse that they suffered in their childhood with their children, or live "half a life," filled with guilt and shame as a result of society's complicit silence, until recently, surrounding the emotionally charged issues of child abuse.

Beverly Potter was well aware of these theories through her irregular contact with child-abuse therapists and women's groups in the past. She was constantly worried that her children were being or would be abused, although her periodic checks with the doctors assured her that her suspicions were misguided. One cannot help but surmise the children must have often heard from their mother that sex was bad, for she was constantly at odds with herself and others over sexuality and personal relationships. It must have been an anxiety-ridden world that the two girls grew up in. Conflict about sexuality no doubt played a major role in the young girls' lives, just as it had always done in their mother's.

With these thoughts in mind, Beverly Potter joined a women's group at the urging of her contact social worker at the Hamilton–Wentworth Children's Aid Society. She would later state that in this group she was able to share her "secrets" with others like her who had suffered their own tragic history. It was the first time, she said, that she had ever told anyone openly about the abuses. Initially she had felt relief over this. Still later, following the allegations of her children, Beverly Potter would accuse the social worker who had convinced her to join the group and had shared in the meetings of betraying her trust by using the information from the group against her in court and other documents. But let's go back and start at the beginning.

Beverly Potter's relationships had always been brief and turbulent. Sarah's father, to whom Beverly had never been legally married, abandoned her for her cousin shortly after the little girl was born. Her second child, Mary, was the product of her marriage to a man who would eventually be tried alongside her, who by then had long since been estranged from her.

Since their separation in 1981, Danny Blake had remained a weekend or "access" parent, carrying on a distant and somewhat stormy, but largely supportive, relationship with the family. The third child, born during this custody battle, was fathered by Beverly's most recent boyfriend, William, who separated from her just as these charges were surfacing. It was an uneasy, unhealthy world, to which the CAS officials did not want the children to return . . . ever.

After the two girls arrived at her home, Jane Wyatt noted in the journal she dutifully kept that the children had been dishevelled, smelling of "urine and semen." Mary had spoken of having bad dreams. On February 22, 1985, two weeks after they arrived, Jane Wyatt informed a CAS worker that she believed the children had been sexually abused. She wrote,

"The signs are easy to detect, but not easy to explain." On February 28, Tricia Donnelly, a Hamilton child sexual abuse expert was called in to assess the allegations. She conducted a second interview a short time later, after which she agreed that sexual abuse had in fact occurred. She noted at the time that she felt that both girls needed a safe and secure environment, and that the older girl would, as a result of her stay, "disclose more information." This report would become extremely important two years later, when the judge made his "finding of fact" concerning the sexual abuse of the children. But at the time it was simply the validating interview that launched this precedent-setting custody battle and enclosed the children in the institutional embrace of the CAS.

During the third week of their stay, the younger child, Mary, allegedly informed Jane that her mother's boyfriend, William, "sticked his fingers in us down there," and demonstrated what she meant by lying down on the floor, spreading her legs, and pointing to her vagina. Within a few days, she was describing how she and her sister were forced to "lick the cream off of his pee thing." A day or two later, Mary, the more vocal of the two girls, went on to say that

> William puts his finger in the poo hole and Mom puts it in there too. Sometimes when we're on the bed, he puts one finger in me and one in my mom, and Mom puts her fingers in me, and Mom sucks. It's so crazy I don't like it. . . . We have Vaseline at our house. . . . We put it in our pee holes and on our bums when they are sore.

This mutual fondling between the children and the adults remained the main theme of the children's allegations throughout the first month of their stay in Jane Wyatt's household.

By the second month of their sojourn, they began to tell of being involved in pornographic videotaping sessions wherein they were forced to participate in group sexual activities that varied from time to time, and that were initiated at the whim of one of the adults, who would routinely sodomize and in other manners sexually abuse them. They stated too that this took place at Hamilton's CHCH-TV studios, where they were allegedly videotaped on numerous occasions. On March 20, while watching television with Jane, Mary stated, "I saw myself on TV with Mom putting her finger in, and I saw William putting his finger in Sarah, and William and Mom and everyone doing those things. . . . There's a tape and they put it in a thing — you know, a thing like a tape-recorder." Sarah turned to her and told her to "keep quiet, not to tell everyone everything." She then turned to the foster mother, "looking embarrassed," and stated that they had been lying, that it was all just dreams. But eventually she too, according to the notes, began opening up to Jane, corroborating the younger girl's graphic tales of molestation, and eventually murder.

"Elizabeth got dead. A killer got her. He had a knife. He was a killer," Mary one day blurted out to Jane. Her sister told her to shut up, as often happened when she spoke of these things. But she wouldn't.

> Me and Mom and William and Mary and Elizabeth went for a drive. Elizabeth was sleeping. We went to the woods. I think she walked. Maybe Mom carried her. She was bad. Mom said she touched things, and they goed in the wood. Mom went in the trees. Her hair is long. Us waited in the car. Mom hurried back from the wood. Mom had blood on her fingers. Mom was scared after a killer got Elizabeth. Mom said she opened her mouth. I guess her mouth opened when the killer got her.

The children allegedly repeated these stories to many different people over a period of three months, during which time the stories became progressively more detailed. Murder and sex were often linked together. Their forced sexual exploits were said to have taken place over many months, during which time objects — and on one occasion, at least, a small animal — were inserted into their vaginas. They would "scream with pain and ask their tormentors many times to stop," but there was no reprieve from their horror. Toward the end of the second month, the girls began speaking of being forced to participate in group sex in graveyards with black-robed adults and other children. Some of the children, they claimed, were murdered and then mutilated. One of the main characters in their evolving drama was a man they called "the Blob": an enormous man with a disfigured face, who would "rip the flesh off of the dead children and cook it up for everybody to eat." Their mother and her boyfriend would also take part "by tearing up the faces and breaking up the hands." They would also, said the older girl, "take home the meat on the plate from the graveyard . . . raw. . . . They cut the meat from the legs above the knees. Everyone eats." Sometimes, Mary confided to their now-captive audience, "When they bury the kids in the graveyard holes we have to go down into the hole and get into the box with all the goo in it. We don't like it. It stinks awful. But we have to do it for the big people or we will be just like the little people in the hole."

Along with these grotesque descriptions of graveyard mutilation and cannibalism, they would draw pictures of little children showing a head in one corner, a torso in another, and feet somewhere off to the side.

Once, while riding in a police car with Jane Wyatt by their side, the children observed the address "666" on a house that they were passing and cowered in fear in the back seat of the car. When asked what was wrong, they said that "the devil" was in there and that he would "come out and get" them for saying what they had been saying, "just as he said he would if we ever told anybody." Was it a coincidence that their grandmother's house was numbered 666 and that this number, 666, is also the "mark of the beast" or the Antichrist in the Bible and derived satanic lore?

The girls' erratic and withdrawn behaviour complemented their stories. Often they would defecate when telling a particularly frightening story. At other times one of the girls would simply stare off into space, becoming oblivious to her surroundings, with a look of stark terror animating her expression. They would tremble, weep, wring their hands in despair, and display other bizarre behavior in keeping with the nature of their disclosures.

The final scathing accusation — which tore the last thread holding these children to their tattered family history — surfaced on May 20, 1985, nearly three months after they arrived at Jane Wyatt's home. After having spent an unsupervised weekend with their father, the girls informed Jane that there was a plot to kill her and her family by the three accused, with their father as the mastermind. The children were nearly hysterical with fear, Jane Wyatt would later tell the court. And so was she. With frightening visions of satanic cult members crawling through her windows in the dead of night and leaving behind a trail of blood and mutilated bodies, Wyatt phoned her support worker and confidant at the Hamilton CAS. A short time later the worker was by her side; together they camped out on the living-room floor. The police immediately supplied protection. Two days later, the Potter girls were whisked away to another foster home and the Wyatt family promptly packed their bags and were moved to a nearby hotel.

It was both the end and the beginning. The children would never repeat their stories with quite the same intensity to the legion of health-care professionals in whose trust they were placed, although the twenty-five hours of videotaped sessions with their therapist offered as evidence in court presented vivid depictions of their traumatized world.

By the end of those first three months, Wyatt's journal ran to more than 170 pages. The world-view of these disturbed children conjured up by reading through the foster mother's notebook was as bizarre and twisted as anything in the annals of Western literature and life.

But it was not simply the content of the document that

would rivet the court during the trial. It was the way the tales evolved — and something else, less definable, but somehow important to what a reader would finally feel about the journal itself, for all its disturbing effect and elaborate detail: in a way that was hard to put a finger on, it seemed that the foster mother and the girls had been involved in what Danny's lawyer, Michael Hartrick, would call a "dynamic of communication" out of which this freak of children's literature emerged. The journal, then — and what it tells us about the progression of the children's stories — is an essential feature of this macabre, precedent-setting Canadian custody battle.

A careful reading of the notebook reveals a number of things that don't make sense. On many pages, Jane Wyatt had scribbled her own comments alongside the children's statements. In one instance she noted that a friend was having a shower that day, which left her "no time to listen" to the children. In a similar vein, she noted some time later that a friend had died and she was attending the funeral. While apparently innocent in and of themselves, these remarks seemed oddly out of place in a journal full of twisted tales of bestiality and ritual murder. On another page she had written "Ernst Lundell" [sic], apparently referring to Ernst Zundel, the neo-Nazi propagandist who was being tried in Toronto at that time for spreading false statements about the Holocaust. The name's connection with her journal entry is not clear.

But what really captures the reader's attention is the foster mother's occasional eagerness to disclose the allegations. She wrote beside a particularly startling piece of information, "Surprise, surprise, surprise"; a later note says, "aha, more secrets." Directly below a comment about graveyard mutilation she had scratched, "just a thought," leaving the reader to wonder whose thought — her own or the children's — she was annotating. Elsewhere, she noted that Sarah was "acting strangely," adding "I know she is hiding something. . . . I know she is terrified" (this last word is written in bold letters scratched into the paper as if by a child trying to match her script to her feelings). One observes too, as the judge later did, a deterioration in the quality of the note-taking, especially during the latter part of the children's three-month stay, when the tales begin to describe the graveyard rituals. Entries become fragmented, cryptic, and excessively depraved: "These wretched death rituals are photographed. . . . Mary is involved. Sexual orgies with the living and the dead. Children partially dismembered. Heads cut off sometimes, other [times] not. . . . Mom breaking children's hands . . . arms cut off . . . penis cut off."

As the tales become progressively more twisted, Wyatt notes: "I am just writing as accurately as I can remember what the children are stating." But other entries indicate that some very dubious editing was going on.

The most baffling and contradictory editorial interventions are Wyatt's cryptic notes and cross-references, which only she herself could translate. These cryptic codes were unscrambled only after the alleged plot to kill her was revealed, at the conclusion of the children's stay. She informed the CAS and the police that these notes referred to the estranged father's involvement in the sexual exploitation of the children. According to her translation, the children had often remarked on the father's involvement, but she felt it was better to leave this out because there were already too many people involved.

This was peculiar, even alarming. The children's explicit statements referring to the father — that is, the uncoded statements that were written in plain English — consistently cast him in a good light. For the greater part of the journal the children, as recorded by the foster mother, had openly and frequently accused their mother, her boyfriend, and other adults of performing all sorts of degrading acts with them, while they portrayed their father as a loving, protective individual who could save them from their horrible plight. Even though he was at that time only an access parent, they spoke of him as someone they could trust. When pressed at one point during one of her numerous subsequent interviews, Sarah blurted out that "the worst part about my father is that he farts": a far cry from the satanic demon conjured up during the girls' last days at Jane Wyatt's.

Admittedly, their idea of a protector — like many of their ideas — was painfully twisted. The younger girl was recorded in early April as saying: "I want Dad to kill William. He has a knife, and I want him to cut Williams' neck. . . . I hate William. . . . I have to call my dad. He has to kill William."

But until the time the plot to kill the foster parents came up and effectively banished him from the girls' new and uncertain life, possibly forever, the CAS had perceived Blake positively: so positively, in fact, that he was allowed unsupervised, though limited, access during the investigation process — a privilege denied the mother and her boyfriend — and serious consideration was given to allowing him custody of the girls if he could demonstrate a suitable home environment.

When asked by defence lawyers why she had kept information about the father to herself — and why she would, in effect, jeopardize the children's safety by placing them in their father's unsafe hands — Wyatt could offer only that she was reluctant to bring any others into the picture since it might damage her already-waning credibility with the police. Judge Beckett eventually decided that the woman had displayed a momentary lapse in judgment due to the stress of listening to the children's graphic descriptions of the hell they had been through. This strains credibility. Surely if she believed the girls' allegations that Blake was a pedophile, a satanic ritual murderer, and a sadist, she wouldn't have allowed the visits. This glaring inconsistency was never satisfactorily explained; it cast a shadow of doubt over the entire journal and the legal proceedings in which it was introduced as evidence.

Based on the assessment of the children when they entered the foster home, the Children's Aid Society and associated health-care workers were bound by law to launch an investigation into whether the parents were capable of providing for the emotional and physical needs of their children. On the basis of the allegations that gradually surfaced during the girls' three-month period at the Wyatts', the CAS brought a motion before the Unified Family Court to remove the children from their parents' custody into permanent Crown wardship, the most extreme form of state intervention into family life in Canada.

Throughout the three-month period that the children remained with the Wyatts, the police had been carrying out their own investigation in conjunction with that of the CAS. They visited houses identified by the children and searched graveyards in both Hamilton and Toronto where some of the alleged abuses were said to have taken place. When they went to CHCH-TV studios in Hamilton, they found that the security and the sophistication of the equipment made secret nighttime access and use virtually impossible. They found no bodies, no mass graves, no mutilated remains of young children — nothing that could substantiate the horrifying experiences the two girls described. Indeed, they found quite the opposite. Children who were said to have been murdered were in fact alive and well, and denied being involved in any way. Police did find a former neighbor of Beverly Potter and her estranged husband's who appeared to fit the description of the "Blob" character, and another child who, while allegedly "terrified" of Potter, nevertheless denied any knowledge of the events that the two girls recounted. But they found no bloodstains, no plates of raw flesh, no freshly turned earthen graves, no satanic paraphernalia, no videotapes — nothing.

At one point, after a day of driving around in Toronto with the police and a social worker, searching in vain for a graveyard that couldn't be found anywhere in the area the girls had indicated, the girls admitted to one of the investigating officers, Sergeant David Bowen, that they had made it all up. "My mom didn't really do it," said the older girl. The CAS did not accept this retraction. According to prevailing doctrines among child-care workers (doctrines that will be examined shortly), abused children regularly retract their statements out of fear of the consequences, due to confusion, or for other reasons. The police, however, eventually became convinced that nothing had happened, that the girls' disturbed world-view had not been shaped by the gruesome events that they were relating to the authority figures around them. How these two children had come to imagine these things, the police were uncertain, but they were convinced that whatever the disturbing cause, the girls had fabricated their stories of satanism and cannibalism. They could not be as certain about the authenticity of the allegations regarding sexual abuse, so they left that for the sexual-abuse investigators — and ultimately the judge — to determine. But as far as they were concerned (at least prior to the revelations about the plot to kill Jane Wyatt and her family), the investigation was closed. They defended that decision after the civil trial concluded, when John Harper, legal representative for the CAS, petitioned to have criminal charges brought against the accused. The police steadfastly maintained that no evidence — certainly not the kind that would satisfy a criminal court — had been or could be found. (No criminal charges were ever, in fact, laid.)

There was one significant aspect of evidence that would have corroborated the girls' tales of the sexual abuse they had allegedly suffered: the medical examination. If, as the girls had claimed, vibrators, small animals, and other objects were inserted into their vaginas and anuses to the point where they were "screaming with pain," there should have been scarred or ruptured hymens — clear evidence of the violation of their bodies. The doctor who examined them at the request of the CAS did in fact write in his report that to the best of his knowledge, the girls had been sexually abused. However, he found *no physical evidence* of abuse. He was convinced not by the evidence but by the reports of the psychological trauma

that the girls seemed to be undergoing. Like any testing procedure, the medical examination is not an infallible method
of diagnosing sexual abuse. But again, the untidy correspondence between what the girls said and what was being discovered in the clinic should have raised questions.

Following the initial disclosures at the foster home, and at
the same time that the police were conducting their investigation, the Children's Aid Society had one of its sexual-abuse
experts interview the children on a number of occasions. The
purpose of the first interview was to provide a safe, secure,
neutral setting for the child, and to provide an opportunity
for the child to make these disclosures for the first time in a
therapeutic environment. The worker also assessed the credibility of the child's stories.

This expert would later inform the court that children
under the age of twelve rarely make up stories of a sexually
abusive nature, and that the younger the child and the more
graphic the detail, the more plausible the disclosures. The
original basis for this premise can be found in the theories of
child psychologist Roland Summit, whose major work — entitled *The Child Sexual Abuse Accommodation Syndrome* — though
extremely controversial, has been championed by a large and
vocal group in the child-welfare field. According to this theory, children will tell their story in bits and pieces, recant,
elaborate, recant again, and demonstrate ambivalent feelings
toward their parental figures.

Child-abuse investigators who subscribe to this school of
thought are extremely wary of allowing an accused parent or
other offender to be present during these sessions. They
argue that the mere presence of the authority figure might
inhibit the child's disclosure, if indeed that person has perpetrated the alleged sexual abuse — and if the child says abuse
took place, then for all intents and purposes the Children's
Aid Society accepts that statement as fact until proven otherwise.

The Hamilton interviewer encouraged the children to make generous use of "anatomically correct" dolls as references, to facilitate difficult statements about the abuse. As a result of her initial interviews with both children, she — along with a second social worker and an investigating police officer, both out of sight in an observation room — decided that the children had been abused.

In later interviews, when the children were reticent to speak, the same expert initiated conversations with comments based upon the allegations that had earlier been made to the foster mother. To refresh the child's memory, or to indicate the kind of information that she was seeking from the child, she would say things like "Mary, who is it that sucks in your family?" (referring to the allegations made to Jane Wyatt earlier, that the children's parental figures had had oral sex with them). The girl replied, "Mommy — I told you." As the interviews proceeded, the girls (especially the younger one) became more and more descriptive in their accounts. After describing a series of fondling maneuvers involving her mother, her mother's boyfriend, and her younger sister in the bedroom, Mary went on to speak of what happened in the bathroom:

> Okay, we're in the bathtub — William, Mom, and me and Sarah, . . . and William goes on top of Mommy, and then on top of me. Then we all change and Mommy goes on top of William and on top of me, and we all kiss, and then they put their fingers in my vagina and it hurts and then they do it to Sarah too, and then to each other. We get to watch. Then I think they get Mom a towel and do something.

(She then demonstrated, using the anatomically correct dolls, how William and her mother would masturbate each other in the bathtub). The interviewer asked what happened next; the young girl replied, "Then William does the same thing to me and he puts his finger in my vagina with the towel. Then he takes it out. Right? . . . 'Cause it gets red. . . . It hurts my vagina."

This interview took place three weeks after the girls arrived at the Wyatts' home, and it convinced the social worker "that what the children were saying was to be believed," and that given a warm and secure environment, the older child — who remained reticent throughout her stay with the foster family — would "disclose more information." Judge Beckett, during the trial, was highly impressed both with the expertise of the sex-abuse investigator and the importance of these particular revelations as they related to his finding as fact that the children had been sexually abused.

This is a difficult decision to uphold. On the one hand, while it is difficult to explain away these kinds of precocious sexual comments by young children, it is not necessarily true that they were based on fact or that no other explanation for their uttering such things was possible.

The Childen's Aid Society and all subsequent authorities involved with these children believed them to have been abused. They did anything they could to assist the girls to disclose what they considered to be terrible secrets. In other words, these two disturbed, needy children were removed from their parental figures and surrounded by authority figures who believed that they had been abused (on the basis of their behaviour, not on what they had said initially), and who attempted to get the children to disclose information about sexual abuse. But as parents who have dealt much with children know, children often tailor their stories to suit what they think adults want to hear. This is perhaps no different from adults who give pollsters or interviewers the answers they want to hear. And it anticipates the central question: did the children repeat and elaborate upon stories that the adults around them wanted to hear, or were they describing their own real and tragic histories of gross sexual abuse?

On February 16, 1985, Jane Wyatt had written, "I think that

the girls have been sexually abused. This is easier to detect than it is to explain." Less than two weeks later the younger girl, who was observed by the foster mother and others to be in need of attention and affection, was telling everyone who would listen how she and her sister had been sexually assaulted. It was felt that the older girl, less willing to speak at first, needed to be worked with over a period of time before she too would "disclose more information." She did, of course — as did the younger girl — detailing a progressively more elaborate labyrinth of degrading sexual acts.

There was no independent assessment of these children — that is, no assessment by an independent team of experts who were not aligned with the Children's Aid Society. The accused adults requested that a team of experts assess them along with the children, but the Society refused, choosing instead to piece together information with independent psychiatrists and other health-care professionals, many of whom had not seen the children and most of whom had not seen both the children and the parents interacting. Normal procedure in such cases is to have the experts observe the members of a family together to gauge the bonding among them.

However, toward the end of the children's stay with the foster parents, a team of experts was called in by the Children's Aid Society to assess the children's statements. This team of sexual-abuse investigators, comprising medical, psychiatric, and other child-care professionals from Toronto's Hospital for Sick Children, assessed the children without the benefit of interviewing them. Relying solely on the allegations reported by the Society and the foster mother, they declared that they could objectively ascertain the truth of the allegations through a formal structural analysis of the statements. However, they noted that this was the first time that this approach had been taken — that is, it was an unproven testing procedure.

More importantly, they believed, even before they started that the children's statements were true. This was made clear during the trial testimony of Dr. Paul Steinhauer, one of the leading experts on the Toronto-based team, who stated explicitly that he could prove the children's statements true without interviewing either the children or their parents. His assertion illustrates what happens to science when conclusions come before facts, rather than being based on fact. In other words, descriptions of events are twisted and construed in order to fit with preconceived ideas. That is bad enough when it happens in science. But the consequences can be worse in law. When something is viewed as true or false prior to coming before the court to be decided upon by the trier of fact, then justice is in grave jeopardy.

All three of the accused people vigorously denied the allegations. They asked for an independent assessment but were refused. They were granted only limited supervised access to the children, and were directed not to mention the allegations on the grounds that to do so would disturb the children. Despite the rhetoric of child-care workers, which would ordinarily cast the adults, too, as victims — in need of help as much as the children — few involved in this case appeared able to perceive Beverly, Danny, and William as anything but villains. They were seen as monsters. Therapeutically, because the children were believed, the adults' maintaining their own innocence was seen as counterproductive, as "refusing to take responsibility for [their] actions." Despite the fact that there was no evidence (apart from statements made by two highly traumatized children — five and seven years old, respectively) to prove or disprove their innocence, the rights of the adults were left in the hands of the Society, whose quasi-judicial authority was even more entrenched in late 1987 by the passing (at least in principle) of Ontario's Bill C-15, which will become the focus of our examination shortly.

By the time the custody battle actually started, the media were no doubt primed to expect the accused to be strange and offensive. But the little group who walked into that crowded

Hamilton courtroom to face one of the most gruelling Family Court trials in Canadian history proved surprisingly anticlimactic: pathetic, perhaps, but not monstrous.

Alone, abandoned once again, Beverly Potter sat down in front of six sterling lawyers, resplendent in their collared robes, and above them — fatherly, sober, silver-haired, and magisterial — the judge. Men were to stand in judgment of her, as they had done throughout her battered life. Her children had become her accusers. Is it any wonder that when she finally broke down under this male-dominated bastion of justice surrounding her, she cried out plaintively, "Please, Daddy. Please leave me alone. I can't take any more"?

She attended the trial nearly every day. She was dressed inappropriately most of the time; she behaved perhaps somewhat "manipulatively," as her husband and others close to her had often contended; possibly she even displayed a "borderline personality disorder" as Hamilton-based psychiatrist Eva Gede submitted to the court; but she was not a monster.

Her estranged husband, Danny Blake, who worked throughout the proceedings as a laborer, showed up infrequently. Danny stood less than 5'6" tall, a wiry, defensive little man. He looked like a furtive squirrel, trapped in a complex story that in his wildest imagination he could not have considered possible. He was straight to the point, unsophisticated, with an aversion to speaking openly of the children's satanic allegations. He called them the other half, setting a trend in the courtroom that was taken up by the lawyers to break the allegations into the sexual and the satanic and refer to the two separately.

He would not speak kindly of his estranged wife. He was openly contemptuous toward her schemes, her goading behavior. When asked if he had ever beaten his wife violently as she had alleged, he questioned the meaning of violence. "Like if you mean do I ever plough her one, no I don't. You don't do that to ladies." Then he hesitated, appearing uncomfortable, confounded. He continued a moment later. "Yeah, I guess I did do that once, but I wasn't awake then. I was asleep and I woke up and there I was driving her right between the eyes, but I was asleep, so you can't blame me for that." It was observed with alarm by all present that this man, who had allegedly threatened to blow away the "whole goddamn army of lawyers," kept in his house or around his person a large knife — Beverly Potter suggested that it was a switchblade — a machete, a meat hook, and a sawed-off shotgun. He admitted once holding a knife to his wife's throat in a fit of rage.

But Danny couldn't explain to the court what might have happened to his children. Violent and ill-tempered he might have been, and he didn't really know how or try to hide that. But the allegations, the kinds of things that allegedly happened to his children, sent a look of horror and pain across his battle-worn face, a look not unlike the hurt of a wounded animal.

William, the father of Beverly's third child, was a quiet-spoken university graduate, indignant that his life and those of his co-accused should be the subject of national discussion and "false accusation." "Until my death," he stated, "these charges will never be true." He seemed an incongruous character in this loathsome drama. He voluntarily submitted to a lie-detector test and a phallometric test in an attempt to prove that he wasn't the kind of person the children allegedly made him out to be. These two tests, along with a battery of other psychological profiles, indicated — according to Dr. Langevin, a world-renowned pedophilia expert from Toronto's Clarke Institute of Psychiatry — that he was normal, not a pedophile, child abuser, criminal, satanist, or any other psychological appellation that fit the kind of person that the children had been describing. He seemed a most unlikely candidate for a child-abuse trial, yet he was the first person to be indicted by the children.

The psychological profiles that came back from independent sources suggested that these adults — while mixed up, sometimes inappropriate, and even (as Dr. Eva Gede submitted, referring specifically to the mother) capable of some "pretty bizarre behavior" — seemed incapable of committing the acts of which they had been accused, which were horrendously bizarre in the extreme. But how, then — and this was the overriding question — could the children come up with these kinds of allegations, with what Judge Beckett often referred to in his summation as "age-inappropriate knowledge" of satanic and sexual behaviors? The police could find no physical evidence of the satanic practices: no missing children, no blood-stained floors, no mass burial sites, no satanic paraphernalia. Nothing. Again, one has to return, as the judge and others did, to the "dynamic of communication" that flowed between Jane Wyatt and the children, because the tormented picture of the world the children conjured up simply didn't fit with any of the facts that came to light.

Judge Beckett's summation, coming after two gruelling years of courtroom drama, is interesting not only because of the way it affected the lives of those on whom he passed judgment, but because it pinpointed the two major problems that this book sets out to address. Judge Beckett found as fact that the children had been grossly emotionally abused, a fact that was fairly evident before the trial began. He found too that they had been sexually abused as they had stated, despite the lack of physical evidence. Judge Beckett's statements regarding this evidence — or rather, this lack of evidence — indicate that, like the Children's Aid Society, he was convinced on the basis of the early disclosures that no one so young could state such things without having prior experience. But his opinion regarding the satanic allegations, which he could not find as fact — while it demonstrated the man's thoughtfulness and the weight of the judgment he was forced to make in this baffling case — leaves unanswered the question of where or how these mind-boggling tales originated. Instead it restates the position of all the experts who testified, who maintained that there was no other plausible explanation:

I am left with the question of where the "florid" [satanic] allegations originated. Was it fantasy? Were the children lying? If the children were fantasizing or lying, the question arises as to where the children got the material to produce their so-called lies or fantasies. I cannot accept that two little children of this age could possibly describe the matters I have described above without some knowledge or some experience in order to create the lies or the fantasies. Such matters surely cannot come out of the minds of young children as native or original thought. But is not the fact that they said such things, that such horrors were in their minds, evidence of a very bizarrely disturbed relationship with their caretakers?

The world of small children is a narrow one: it is mother, it is father, and their families, their school, and their playmates. It is in this milieu that a child's mental constructs are moulded. What experiences did these children have while in the care of the adults involved that would cause them to say what they said and to say it with such fear and terror? To say that they "lied" or that it was "fantasy" falls far short of explaining how such things could have been in their minds. . . .

It is not necessary to make findings of fact with respect to those allegations in order to determine whether the children are in "need of protection" within the meaning of the legislation.

It is quite clear that the majority of the child psychologists who appeared at the trial believed, on the basis of the children's words alone, that what they said was true. Judge Beckett, in fact, indicated that in these experts' zeal to establish the credibility of the evidence they had overstepped their bounds. "Their opinions," he stated, "went to the ultimate issue that the court must decide: i.e., is what these children said to be believed?" They had decided a priori that it was.

This was an extremely important determination for the judge to make; it countered experts in the volatile field of developmental psychology.

Following the lead of their U.S. child-protection counterparts, Children's Aid Society officials repeated the dogma that children do not lie. This dogma — which has spread throughout the U.S. and is most clearly expressed by child psychiatrist Roland Summit (referred to earlier in this chapter) — gives diagnostic certainty to a cluster of symptoms that allow one to tell if a child has been abused. According to this theory, when children say that they have been abused, we can be certain that they have been — period. They simply do not lie about such things. Summit claims that this theory is based on the pattern of disclosures that he and other practitioners have seen during their work with incestuous families. Summit's theories have gained tremendous support from social workers and a coalition of psychiatrists and pediatricians whose main aims are to reduce the incidence of child sexual abuse; to educate society about the issue of sexual abuse (one that they believe the public tends to trivialize); and to establish support systems for the victims of sexual abuse. It is largely the result of Summit's work that the "children-don't-lie" school of thought has had such a strong impact on the manner in which North American society now deals with sexual abuse. To the proponents of this theory, the stranger and more lurid the abusive situation described by the child, the more difficult it would be for the child to fabricate it; therefore, the more likely it is to be true.

This belief greatly simplifies courtroom procedure. If children don't lie, then no corroborative evidence is needed to verify their claims of abuse. The assumed veracity of their accusations also means that children need not be challenged or cross-examined in the usual courtroom manner. This has been seen as a giant step forward in the fight against child abusers — who, in the past, were able to continue their abuse of powerless children because children could not testify against them without evidence. But as progressive as this principle sounds, it has created a situation rife with the potential for a dizzying number of false accusations of child abuse, resulting in excruciatingly long — and, in the end, pointless — trials. For the contention itself is by no means certain, as other child development psychologists, as well as simple common sense, will attest. Children *do* lie. They absorb far more than adults often realize from television, their peers, advertisements; from their own inner storehouse of fact and fantasy, they can create a rich and varied fantasy world. The Hamilton trial thus highlighted a crucial issue, which will be examined in Chapter 2. the academic controversy over the correct way to conceptualize children's minds.

This leads immediately to a second major problem. If mental-health or child-care professionals can invoke police and judicial authorities on the uncorroborated testimony of children, they are then acting in a quasi-judicial manner that approaches dangerously close to the responsibility of the courts to decide guilt or innocence. If everyone automatically believes that the abuse occurred, they must act as though the accused are guilty. They have, in effect, as Judge Beckett noted with respect to the Toronto team of experts, already determined something that should be left to the trier of fact — the judge — to decide. Believing the alleged offender to be guilty, they must limit that person's access to the child. They must in effect make the kinds of decisions affecting the child's life that are ordinarily regarded as the prerogative of parents.

This fundamental breach of the centuries-old presumption of innocence principle will also be examined at length in Chapter 2. But it can be stated here that if this method of legal proceedings is accepted, the judicial system is open to serious abuse. For instance, separated parents may use the courts and child-abuse allegations as a weapon in their postmarital warfare. If a charge of sexual abuse is brought against a parent during an access visit, the child is immediately removed from the suspected offender's home, the case is jointly investigated by the police and the CAS, and the alleged offender is frequently forced to go through the courts to prove his or her innocence.

During the time between the arousing of the CAS's suspicions and the judge's assessment of fact, an accused offender will see the child on a very limited, supervised basis, if at all. Even if the judge feels that no abuse can be proven to have taken place, he or she is often still wary of sending the child back into the suspected abuser's environment without a stringent set of conditions.

Are officials of a body such as the Children's Aid Society really capable of making decisions regarding when the state should intervene in the lives of its citizens?

About this particular trial, some would argue that justice was done. None of the accused adults will ever have access to these children again. So the children may well be better off now than they would have been in their unstable, chaotic home. But it seems to me that this trial raised more questions than it answered, and cast grave doubts over the legal rights of individuals accused of child abuse. Why grant the Children's Aid Society such authority? Why were the psychiatrists unanimously agreed, despite the fact that there was no evidence to support the children's claims of bestiality, murder and Satanism? And finally, how do science, especially psychiatry/psychology (where disagreement is acknowledged and, indeed, considered necessary for the furtherance of knowledge) and justice (where there can be only one viewpoint acknowleged) — how do these two systems of human endeavor meet in the troubled context of human sexual behavior?

2
A LEGAL DILEMMA:
The Line Between Fact and Fantasy

**Then they took me and my wife inside and locked us up.
From that day we never saw our kids again for nine months.**
Tom Brown, Scott County trial, Jordan, Minnesota, 1985

Until very recently, society in general, like Freud, refused to believe that more than a very few children were routinely victimized and brutalized — not just in the context of satanists or other cultists, but that they were abused at all. Contributing to this state of affairs was the fact that many abused children, though not all, came from poorer socioeconomic backgrounds and had no recourse for complaint and only minimal protection from their parents or official guardians. Even when they spoke, nobody listened. But during the last several decades an army of child advocates has risen up to defend the rights of children to have freedom from physical, emotional, and sexual abuse.

The various defensive measures that these advocates use, including interviewing techniques, methods of interrogation, and sexual-abuse investigation teams, result directly from the theory espoused by Roland Summit and his zealous colleagues. And somehow, despite numerous instances where these well-intentioned child advocates have been proven wrong, and despite the damage this psychological theory has inflicted on unsuspecting families and communities, these ideas are gaining popularity, and have kindled a moral panic that has spread into the legal, medical, psychiatric, and general realms. The courts have come to rely more and more on the testimony of "expert" health professionals, who in turn argue for the infallibility of children's statements.

Consider the following example of psychiatry entering the courtroom:

In 1985, a twenty-nine-year-old California man was accused of molesting his two daughters, aged three and four. The father vigorously maintained his innocence. At one point a child-abuse expert, who teaches police and child-protection workers how to determine if a child has been molested, was testifying regarding the importance of the father taking responsibility for his behavior, and on why he shouldn't be allowed to see his daughters until he did so. The judge eventually intervened.

> Hold on a minute. Let's assume, for the sake of this question, that the adjudication is favorable to the father and that the truth of the allegation is not established. Are you indicating then that the children should have no further contact with him, that it would be harmful to the children to see their father if the court finds that events that are alleged have not been sufficiently established?

"Yes, your Honor," the expert replied.

The judge, perplexed, asked again, "You mean, if judged innocent, the children should have no further contact with their father?"

"Yes," the expert maintained.

The attorney who had called this witness commented to the judge, "I think she must have misunderstood, your Honor." The expert broke in and said, "No: in terms of . . . the emotional health of a child who has said [that abuse] has occurred and [that] this is what happened in this case, it would be very disturbing for a child to have contact with the parent who is saying, 'No, what happened, what you said, is not true.' "

Her own attorney then asked her, "What if it didn't happen?" — to which she replied, "Whether or not this particular issue can be proven in a court of law, you know, I can't comment upon that. What I can say is that in my opinion there isn't any question about that."[1]

The judge dismissed this expert, obviously upset by her arrogance and wanton disregard for the need for evidence to back up the claims. But this witness and her theories are not unique. She was simply applying a maxim that is widely accepted by child-abuse intervention counsellors and investigators: children do not fabricate sexual-abuse stories. Why take the word of the court, this expert was saying, when you have the word of the child?

This naive reliance on children's testimony has resulted in an alarming increase in the number of unfounded child-abuse reports and investigations. Because, of course, children *do* lie. A child's malleable psyche exists on the borderline between fact and fantasy, a fantasy filled with richly detailed sexual imagery that can become, for a child, as "real" as fact, if reinforced by well-meaning but misguided adults.

But to point to the theories of Summit or Susan Sgroi (one of the most devoted, articulate, and influential members of the children-don't-lie school of thought) as the instigators of the present rash of sexual-abuse cases is not to dismiss their endeavors out of hand. Child abuse is a real, horrifying problem, and many children are in danger. For such children, child advocates play a significant, supportive role. And since we are dealing here with the delicate minds of children, with the harsh realities of child abuse, and with the novel concern for children's rights, we need to proceed with caution. But the fact that hundreds of thousands of innocent people are having their reputations tarnished and their privacy invaded because of poorly substantiated child-abuse claims may cre-

ate a backlash against efforts to help children who have suffered very real abuse.

This alarming trend toward trying child-abuse cases on
largely uncorroborated evidence took nearly a decade to
develop in the U.S. As the trials proceeded, one case after
another appeared to break down. For this, prosecutors
blamed the fact that they could not properly interview the
children, given uncertain laws regarding child testimony, and
a genuine reluctance to put children through any more emotional stress than was caused by the original trauma. Social
workers and child psychologists blamed a system that refused
to listen to children. Police and investigating authorities,
including the FBI, suggested that there simply wasn't enough
evidence to make the bulk of the charges stick. None of this, of
course, could redeem the already messed-up lives of the families who were pulled into these "witch-hunts," as one victim
called them (using an analogy that would be used over and
over to describe what happened to those on trial for child
abuse during the closing decades of the twentieth century).
These judicial foul-ups have reached such proportions in the
U.S. that an association has been formed under the banner
"Victims of Child Abuse Laws" (VOCAL). A national group
comprising parents who have been falsely accused and professionals who represent them, VOCAL publishes a national
newsletter and boasts more than 3,000 active members in
nearly 100 chapters. They lobby governments, initiate peti-
tions, and help with the legal and emotional problems caused
by the disruptive investigatory procedures of child-protection workers.

This chapter will examine in some detail several massive
trials that left entire communities — and even entire states —
in a welter of moral dilemmas and social confusion.

Dr. Ralph Underwager is one of the few who dissents from
the prevailing children-don't-lie doctrine. A Minnesota-based
child psychologist who has been called to testify about children in more than twenty states, he suggests that in the inter-

rogations of children, care-givers are tapping into the fantasy lives of their young charges. He believes that normally adults act as a sort of check on a child's fantasy life, but that, in the frightening, topsy-turvy world of police investigations and court trials, we have abandoned this role, and given rein to these fantasies. It is as if we have climbed into the closet with them and told them that the "bogeyman" is real and that he is going to get them. Children, Underwager admonishes, are highly suggestible, and the kinds of leading questions that are routinely asked by child advocates actually implant a desired response. And as will be obvious in the cases described below, many adults will not stop asking questions until they get the desired answer. Over and over, children are grossly manipulated into uncovering what for them may seem to be a frightening reality, but what is, in fact, a projection of a programmed or prompted fantasy onto the darkness around them.

But Underwager does not believe that all children's testimony is without any foundation in fact. "Reality," he says, "even a child's reality, can be tested. It is quantifiable. The aim of psychology is to test reality and approach as close to the truth as is possible for science. Children's statements can be assessed to see how close [those] statements fit with the reality around them. This is the goal of psychology as regards the assessment of sexual abuse claims by children."[2] His suggestions have not made him very popular. Underwager and a handful of other psychiatrists and psychologists are calling into question the dangerously naive attitudes of child-abuse investigators.

Underwager's testimony has in some cases resulted in a careful examination of the evidence, thereby leading to a dismissal of charges against the accused. Where a trial continues, this careful examination of the evidence often results, not surprisingly, in acquittal. Unfortunately, the damage to the child, the family, and often the community will already have taken its toll.

The difficulty, of course, lies in discerning *when* children are telling the truth and when they are not — which, to a large degree, can be determined only through corroborative evidence. The prerequisite that children's testimony be corroborated by other evidence has been standard practice in Canadian and American criminal courts for decades. In many of the present ritual murder/gross sexual-abuse cases, however, the corroborating evidence is often shaky or nonexistent. But, with the children-don't-lie battle cry sounding in their ears, sexual-abuse investigators have tended to disregard the flimsiness of the evidence, or the complete lack of it, and in some cases have convinced a judge to do so as well.

For instance, children have stated that they were shunted away by helicopter on a daily basis and forced to participate in sex orgies in another state, then returned by the end of their school day to be picked up by their mothers.[3] According to some children, the sexual abuse they detail had been happening for years. Upon hearing such "evidence," sex-abuse investigation teams comprising police and social workers trained in the children-don't-lie school have arrested scores of adults. But in most instances, they failed to ask quite obvious questions before acting. Would it not seem natural that someone, somewhere, would have seen a helicopter and marked its flight path and passengers? And if gross sexual abuse were happening on a regular basis, as was maintained by many children, why would parents not be told about it for months, even years, and how could they fail to notice something unusual about their children's behavior? Is it even conceivable that at the end of day, a mother asking her child "So what did you do today, Debra?" would be told nothing about airplanes, helicopters, and other significant, exotic, or painful events, or that her child's behavior would be completely normal after months and even years of abuse?

There are more questions to ask in this regard, and we will pose them later; for now it can be stated unequivocally that children do fabricate wild and richly detailed stories and can be pressured into embellishing those stories for interested

authority figures. Yet many adults have believed these allegations and have used them to prosecute other adults despite
denials and a complete dearth of evidence. A few cases are
undoubtedly true, but in our zeal to prosecute suspected
abusers, we may have lost sight of the care needed in discerning truth from fantasy in the mind of a child, and of the
limitations to our own ability to discern guilt and innocence.

"Young children were forced by their daycare workers [to]
join in sexual orgies with the living and the dead, and were
then forced to eat the flesh of dismembered bodies" read a
headline in the Sacramento *Bee*. A similar message, with
minor variations, has rocked upwards of forty communities
across North America since late 1983.

In January 1984, authorities in Sacramento and Campbell,
California, rounded up five men and accused them of partici-
pating in a series of satanic sexual rituals with more than a
dozen children. Prosecutor Rick Lewkowitz induced the
court to set bail at $500,000 by telling the judge that there was
"evidence" that three of the youngsters involved had been
killed and that the men had filmed the slayings. The media
dubbed this the "snuff film child molestation case." The public was outraged.[4]

All five accused men were jailed. They were labelled as
child abusers and treated as such by jailers and prisoners.
One of them was beaten by fellow inmates. Their families,
well-known and respected members of the community until
this time, were ostracized and received threats.

Then, over the course of a few nightmarish months, the
case, as one attorney put it, began "falling apart at the seams."

A polygraph test was given to one of the accused, John Paul
Holman, an acquaintance of Gary Dill, the father of the children who had made the initial accusations. Holman insisted,
as had all the accused, that he was innocent, and the polygraph test bore him out. As is common, the test, was not
allowed as evidence in court, but it nevertheless convinced a

number of people of his innocence. In April, nearly four months after the case began, the judge dropped the bail for the accused from $500,000 to $10,000. These men had spent three full months in jail, separated from their families and reviled by their community; they had been fired from their jobs, and were still tainted with the possibility of guilt. Four days later, when the last of the 169 felony counts that could have sent each to prison for more than 300 years was dismissed by municipal court Judge Ronald Robie, all five men were set free.

At the time of this writing, one lawsuit had been filed and others were pending against various officials, including Lewkowitz and District Attorney John Dougherty, for what the freed men say was "prosecution in the extreme." This is the gist of the coverage the national media gave the story. But the real story is much more revealing, disturbing, and typical of these kinds of cases.

How did the case get started? Testimony and documents suggest that the criminal case grew from a seed planted in late 1983 by Doris Bell of Vallejo, California, grandmother of one of the young "victims."

Bell's oldest daughter, Claudia, was married to Gary Dill, thirty-four. The marriage had just been shattered by his departure from the family home in Fresno. He had gone to live with a man, his estranged wife would later testify, and was not adequately supporting the family. Claudia's mother had offered to let Claudia and Gary's two daughters stay with her because Claudia was incapable of providing for them alone.

Bell was, by her own admission, obsessed with incest. She had written a 327-page unpublished manuscript, "The Terrible Thing That Happened To Dolly," an account of her personal struggle to relieve a daughter of a "secret" she had carried for many years. Apparently, Bell had discovered, four years after her husband's death, that he had repeatedly molested their daughter. She later testified in court that she too had been a victim of incest. As a child she was "raped by

[her] brother," she said. She claimed to have retaliated in kind: "Two of my female cousins and I got my brother isolated and we molested him." In an effort to deal with this and similar problems, Bell joined a group that included incest survivors and mothers of incest victims.

She had attended some forty meetings of the group in Oakland, California, and found comfort in the fact that she wasn't alone. She felt that others would find the same comfort if they could only be brought to speak about it and deal with the problem. When asked to characterize her interest in incest and child sexual abuse in late 1983 (when the children came to live with her), she replied that the subjects were her "primary occupation."

During the months that followed the move to Mrs. Bell's house, the two young girls came to hate it there.

According to Bell the children exhibited anti-social behavior — bickering, fighting, and not allowing each other their own space. Bell called such behavior "acting out," and believed that it implied that the girls had secrets that they wanted to tell but were unable to express verbally. Their bad behavior was their way of letting Bell and their mother know this. She wasted no time in prying the secrets out of them.

The first revelations came on Easter Sunday, three months after the children had arrived. Under Bell's "interrogation," the children admitted that their father had molested them on several occasions. But Bell thought there was more. The two girls revealed during the course of the trial that over a period of several months they were forced to endure interrogation sessions with their grandmother that lasted up to four hours. They later admitted that they feared their grandmother and were pressured by her to keep telling the story to investigators. They suggested that their grandmother was getting back at their father for leaving them stranded.

Bell denied the children's accusations. She also testified that she used conjecture and theory to draw from her grandchildren the "secrets" of sexual abuse. In another unpublished treatise, "On Establishing Trust with Incest Victims", she had exhorted her readers to pry the secrets out of victims of molestation: "Don't ask permission. Just do it." Bell felt the children were benefitting from the sessions because they were finally being relieved of their terrible burden.

Using amateurish psychological guidelines that she later said were developed from her own experience, Bell suggested that you should "expect that the extent of the exploitation is far greater than you at first imagine. Form an idea of what the child wants to say and then offer that as an explanation." As an example she cited how she got the children to talk about their involvement in cannibalism and mutilation: "I told their mother that the children didn't look relieved as children would be if the secret was out so I suggested that the secret had to do with cannibalism and mutilation of bodies." Until this point she had been suggesting only rape and murder. She asked the child, "Now tell me honestly, did you have to eat the parts of the bodies of the children after cutting them in pieces?" The child, she claimed, "was tremendously relieved at this point."

Other children were brought into the affair by the Dill children at Bell's insistence. At first the other children denied involvement, but when pressured by police and social workers, they admitted that they too had been molested. Accusations escalated — from mere fondling, the children progressed to penetration, then ultimately to murder, mutilation, and cannibalism. One child told the court that murders did occur and that she was forced to commit one of the killings herself (she was six years old when she testified and four years old at the time of the alleged murders). She later admitted lying to please her inquisitors. "The only people who ever seen me without my clothes on are my mom and dad," she finally blurted out. Asked why she had said all these things, she answered that "he [referring to the police officer] was telling me what to say and I just said it. I was too scared to tell him the truth."

During the course of their investigation, the police could find no evidence of dead bodies or even missing children to match the children's accounts. None of the accused had a history of sexual abuse. And all of the children, when given the opportunity, recanted their stories during the course of the trial.

The Dill children were allowed to testify via videotapes. They told attorneys from both sides that neither their father nor anyone else had molested them sexually.

"Then why did you say such things and for so long?" the seven-year-old girl was asked by the defence attorney.

" 'Cause our grandmother made us," the child replied. "She wouldn't let us out of the house unless we said it was true."

Dill's attorney, E.F. Winters, asked the little girl if her grandmother, Doris Bell, was mean to her.

"Yes," came the quick reply.

He then asked if the grandmother ever made up strange stories. The girl's eyes grew wide and she replied emphatically, "Yes".

But the trial had not been the first time the children had denied the abuse stories. After enduring months of interrogation at Bell's home, the children, at the state's insistence, were admitted to MacCauley Institute, a neuropsychiatric treatment center not far from their home. During their thirteen months there, and even during the course of the trial, when they attempted to tell their therapist that their stories weren't true, the therapist interpreted this as part of the denial stage of the Summit's "child sexual abuse accommodation syndrome."

The methods that had been used to wrest information from the children involved interrogation, manipulation, and marathon confessional sessions. Like the medieval inquisitors who had a set of characteristics for identifying a witch that were imposed on any accused person, child-abuse investigators have a fairly specific set of expectations developed around the abuse that children suffer. This is precisely the pattern that Underwager identified in over seventy cases.[5]

Doris Bell's conscious manipulation of her grandchildren represents one of the more primitive attempts to wrest a supposed secret from children. But it demonstrates how an overly zealous committment to protecting children from abuse can infect child-protection teams, law enforcement officers, and others involved in civil or criminal procedures. The therapists at the MacCauley Institute were describing what was, to the best of their knowledge, a symptom of sexual abuse. The behavior of suspected victims of sexual abuse, once they have been labelled as such, is understood by those working with them in the light of that "abuse." Nothing the supposed victim says or does can weaken that conviction. No one knows what effect this labelling of the children as victims will have on the children in the long run.

If this were the only case to come before the courts in North America, we could look upon it as a minor tragedy and hope that in some way the families and children are able to reshape their disrupted lives. But the number of such cases is escalating: different actors, different children, and different prosecutors, but the same zealous script, the same labelling of victims, the same lack of evidence, the same questionable child testimony, and the same community panic.

In California, seventy-six-year-old Virginia McMartin ran what was widely considered to be the best preschool in Manhattan Beach. That was before the fateful day in 1983 when the first of 115 charges of sexual abuse were levelled against her and her staff, one of whom was her son. Seven people were arrested and imprisoned. The children involved in the abuse followed the classic pattern of such disclosures, describing first fondling, then ritual sex, then murder. The trial continues as this book goes to press, though five of the original accused have been released for lack of evidence, and a prosecutor in the case has resigned over what he feels was a miscarriage of justice. He informed the media that there was never enough evidence to bring these people to trial in the first place. The children have admitted that they made up the stories after repeated attempts by abuse investigators to get them to admit to being molested.

But the case, of Bob and Lois Bentz, is probably the best-known in this category. This story highlights how crucial civil liberties can be violated by shoddy investigative procedures, and is typical of the ordeals many VOCAL members have undergone — their lives radically interrupted, in many cases ruined — after being falsely accused of child abuse. The tragedy is made bearable only by the Bentzes' strength in the face of adversity and by Lois's courageous decision to go public with her own and others' stories.

Bob and Lois had two young sons when they moved out of Minneapolis and bought a bungalow that nestled into a hill on the outskirts of Jordan, Minnesota. "I just hated living in the city," said Lois. "I wanted to bring the children up in the country. And Jordan reminded me of the small town where I'd grown up in Wisconsin. You know, you go down to the gas station and they'd do all the little extras for you — check the water, check the tires. Small-town hospitality. I liked that and I wanted my children to grow up in that atmosphere."

Life in Jordan turned out pretty much the way the Bentzes' had hoped. They had a third son. All the boys had plenty of room to ramble on their two-and-a-half acre property and the couple had no trouble making friends in town. Bob would drive to his job in the paint department at the Ford plant in St. Paul, some forty miles away, and when the boys were all old enough to go to school, Lois got an evening job at a local printing plant.

On October 3, 1983, a twenty-six-year-old garbage collector named James Rud, who lived at the Green trailer park in Jordan, was arrested and charged with thirteen counts of sexual abuse against four children. Rud, a quiet-spoken, insignificant-looking man, had a record of child molestation. In 1979, while he was serving in the army, he had been given a one-year suspended sentence for similar offences, and in 1980, after being arrested for fondling two girls under 13, he was sentenced to ninety days in jail and five years' probation.

Among the Bentzes' friends were Tom and Helen Brown, a couple who lived nearby, and whom they had known for eight years. Lois didn't pay attention to the local molestations until Helen's sister, Chris, who also lived at the trailer park, was arrested and charged with ten counts of sexual abuse. "I was stunned," said Lois, "but I kind of thought 'no smoke without fire.' "

Tom and Helen had also moved to Jordan from Minneapolis. Tom had a good job repairing trailers, and Helen was a cook at the truck stop. "My sister was the one that turned Rud in," said Helen. "I was down at the station when her kids gave their statement. I was mad. As far as I'm concerned, no one has the right to abuse kids."

When Helen's sister was arrested, the Browns put up their house for bail to get her out, and they applied to the court to get custody of Chris's children, who had been put into foster care. They were still waiting for word on the home study that would determine if theirs was a fit place for the children to live when, on January 11, Helen noticed several police cars parked on her street as she brought her eight-year-old daughter home from a doctor's appointment. "I knew most of the policemen, and I smiled and waved," she said. "I wondered what was going on, but I didn't think it concerned me."

A short time later, she looked out of the window and saw even more police cars outside the house. When she opened her door to the police a few minutes later, they told her she was under arrest for sexually molesting seven children and that her daughter and her ten-year-old son would be taken into foster care. She would later recall:

They told me to pack the clothes for the kids. I kept

saying, "You've got the wrong Helen Brown." And I was crying and the kids were crying and they were holding on to me. And then, before I knew it, they had taken [away] my kids and their clothes . . . . And then they put handcuffs on me out in the yard in front of all the neighbors and put me in the back of the squad car and took me to Shakopee. When I got there they took my fingerprints and my mug shot, and they put me in a little square cell. It was about 5′ by 5′, with just a toilet and a sink and a light and a thin mattress to sit on. And then they took me over to Carver County jail and put me in there and I don't know how it is with other ones, but they make you get undressed in front of a woman or a man or whichever. With me it was a woman. They tagged my clothes, and they checked my body for I don't know what. Then I had to go over and pick up my mattress and my sheets and carry [them] over and make up my bed. I felt so dirty. I don't undress in front of anybody. I never have and probably never will. And so when I got put in my cell I was crying and they had a TV and I turned it on and there's my husband's picture and our house on TV. It was very humiliating. You feel degraded. You feel dirty to be even associated with something as horrifying as that. And all you keep thinking is, "my kids, what are they doing with my kids?"

Tom Brown had been at work at the Ford plant when he received a call saying that if he wanted to see his kids again he had better get down to the police station right away. " 'We're bringing your wife in now,' " Brown remembers being told. He continues, "I was there before they got there, and when they came up they asked right away if my wife was guilty and I said, 'No, she is not.' Then they took me and my wife inside and locked us up. From that day we never saw our kids again for nine months."

The Browns' arrest came as a shock to the Bentzes. "They

were our neighbors," says Lois. "We would be in each others' houses. Our kids would be playing together all the time. That's when we realized something was wrong. We didn't doubt their innocence for a minute."

They may have had just a moment of doubt during these troubled and troubling times, for no parent is without doubt in such circumstances. A few days after their friends' arrest, the Bentzes and their three boys (then aged twelve, nine, and five) watched "Something About Amelia," a television movie about a girl abused by her father. "Well, we sat the kids down and asked them if they'd been touched wrong," said Lois. "The little one told us that his friend Jeff beat him up. I said no, not that. And then I talked to them alone and Bob talked to them alone, and we came to the conclusion that everything was fine."

That night the Bentzes, along with about thirty other friends of the Browns, appeared before the town council to protest what was going on. A few days later Bob was quoted in the local paper as saying he didn't like the way people were being treated. In particular he objected to the fact that the TV stations were being tipped off even before the people themselves knew they were about to be arrested. Speaking up, it turned out, was a mistake.

The following night, while Lois was at work, the police called at home: they wanted to interview the Bentz children. Lois refused because she knew that in previous cases the parents had been arrested before having another chance to see their children. The next day, the Bentzes found a lawyer — who, after interviewing their children, assured the couple that they had nothing to worry about.

That afternoon Bob, who normally arrived home a few minutes before the boys, had to work overtime. At 5:20 p.m., Lois received a phone call at work from the Scott County sheriff's office. "We've been to your house," an officer told her. "We've got the kids. Take your time, get hold of your husband, and drive yourself down here." The couple, he said, would be charged with criminal sex abuse. "Park a couple of blocks away," he added. "The media are here."

An hour before, Lois had recounted to her foreman, Harry, the strange recent happenings in Jordan. "I put the phone down and grabbed Harry. I was just shaking so hard. I was crying. I said, 'Harry, they're arresting me and Bob. This is crazy.'"

The Bentzes would later learn from their neighbors that four squad cars had pulled up outside their home with a large force of deputies and social workers. After ordering the boys to get their clothes together, this crew had then searched the house from top to bottom.

Lois had already told the boys that strange things might happen and, if they did, not to worry, because Mom would take care of it. "I remember the day before it happened, the youngest came home with an ear infection and I bought him this little stuffed Garfield cat he'd wanted. I remember look-ing at him sleeping on the sofa with Garfield nestled up next to him and thinking, God, what would I do without him? What if someone took mine away?"

When Bob and Lois arrived at the police station, the media and the police were waiting for them. "We are the latest in the Jordan witch-hunt," Lois told the deputy officer who arrested her.

The nightmare had begun.

America had indeed not seen anything like this since the McCarthy era, or perhaps since frightening events that took place in Salem, Massachusetts. But to the people of Scott County, this was not a distant historical event from a textbook; these were their own lives that were being affected. During the winter and spring of 1983/84, suspicion spread like a medieval plague through Jordan, followed by accusations and arrests. Even to talk to the wrong person was to risk contami-nation. When Tom and Helen Brown were released on bail, they couldn't face the prospect of returning to an empty house. They went to stay with a couple in their fifties, Duane and Dee Rank. Shortly thereafter, the Ranks too were arrested and charged with criminal sexual conduct.

At one point in November 1983, arrests were being made on a daily basis. Rud's parents were picked up, along with his girlfriend. Even the law enforcement agencies now scooping up suspects were not above suspicion. In February 1984, Gregg Myers — a quiet, church-going member of the Jordan police force — was arrested and charged with criminal sexual conduct. Three months later, his wife, Jane, was also arrested.

That came as a shock to Don Buchan, a thirty-seven-year-old Scott County sheriff's deputy, and his wife, Cindy. The Buchans attended the same church as the Myerses — St. Paul's Lutheran. Cindy had recently started a part-time secretarial job and Jane babysat their three children. They got along famously. Surely, they couldn't be child abusers too, thought Don. Cindy suggested that they call the county attorney, whom Cindy had known for a couple of years: perhaps she would help them understand what was going on. Her name was Kathleen Morris.

Morris, two years out of law school when she was elected county attorney, was an intense and emotional woman. Divorced and without children of her own, she had taken it upon herself to save the sexually abused children of Scott County. "I take it personally when we can't save a child," Morris was quoted as saying in *People* magazine, where she would be spotlighted as one of the "most intriguing people" of 1984. And in James Rud, Kathleen Morris found the instrument with which she thought she could pry open a Pandora's box of unimaginable horrors occurring in Jordan.

Rud had originally been charged with thirteen counts of sexual abuse. Later eighty-five more were added. As a confessed child molester, he faced more than forty years in prison. Morris had a deal to offer him. Forget about the forty years, she suggested. She could get him into St. Peter's State Hospital for treatment. All he had to do was come up with the names of other child molesters in the community. At first Rud refused, but then it must have occurred to him that this would be a cinch. He turned out a 113-page statement in which he implicated eighteen of the twenty-four people who would eventually be arrested in Jordan.

Kathleen Morris was only too happy to help Cindy. She suggested that the Buchans bring in their oldest daughter. The child was interviewed by Morris, by a social worker, and by an investigation officer. Two days later, despite that team's inability to find any evidence of child abuse, the Buchans were arrested. No explanation was given. Don was simply asked to turn in his gun; he was informed that he and Cindy stood accused of sexually abusing the Myerses' two children, as well as the oldest Buchan daughter.

As they booked him, Don Buchan thought, "Jesus, have they screwed this one up. But give them a day or two; they'll check it out and that will be the end of it." He'd given a statement and offered to take a lie-detector test. He was never given one by the investigators although he later took one on the advice of his attorney; he passed it. The Buchans were taken to the nearby Carver County jail and locked in cells alongside each other. They were not allowed to communicate, but Don could hear Cindy crying all night. The next day, when he was taken from his cell briefly, he caught a glimpse of her. "She was in real bad shape," he recalled. "I'm not even sure that she recognized me."

When Don Buchan was arrested, the arresting officer told him immediately that if he would co-operate in implicating others in the purported child sex ring, he and Cindy would serve no time at all in jail, and the county would pay to relocate the whole family. He hoped at the time that the whole thing was a nightmare, and he would wake up and forget about it in the morning. It was worse than a nightmare: he could wake up, but it wasn't going to go away.

Officers and social workers had meanwhile picked up the Buchans' youngest child at the babysitter's and taken him to a foster home, while Kathleen Morris had driven their two daughters to another foster home. This was not unusual: as more and more children were scooped up, Morris frequently ferried around carloads of children — perhaps she saw herself as a den mother or guardian angel. She also involved herself intimately in the investigation, acquiring her own set of anatomically correct dolls for use when interrogating children about how they had been abused.

Much later, the parents would discover that untrained social workers and police officers had used such dolls in a rather unorthodox fashion when they interrogated the children. If the children didn't respond, the interrogator would take off the dolls' clothes and put them together in various poses, asking, "Did she do this?" or "How about this?" In some cases the investigations would go on for weeks, with Morris, social workers, police officers, even foster mothers taking turns badgering the children into admitting they had been abused. Only after exhaustive questioning would the children be taken to a psychologist, who was always given the impression that the children were being interviewed for the first time.

By June 1984, Jordan had become virtually synonymous with sex abuse across the United States. Newspapers everywhere carried reports of the scandal. *Us* magazine ran the headline: "Justice in Jordan: Amid a nationwide outcry, an outraged prosecutor makes child abusers unwelcome in Jordan." It was, said the article, "the largest case of its kind ever uncovered in Minnesota." From Dade County, Florida, to Staten Island, New York, sexual-abuse investigators praised the courageous prosecution team that refused to allow molesters, no matter how respectable they appeared, to remain at large. For a time — a brief but damaging time — it was a model investigation.

Scott County Attorney Kathleen Morris was a crusader. She believed fervently in what she was doing. She said in an interview that "when you look at . . . abused [children] their eyes don't sparkle. They are basically dead. But once you get them into a foster home their lives improve immediately. They start believing that maybe Mommy and Daddy won't hurt [them] any more, and that's exactly what we want to hear." She certainly did get exactly what she wanted to hear from the kids — initially.

When the first case — that involving Lois and Bob Bentz — came to trial in the nearby town of Chaska in 1984, everyone involved expected a quick conviction. Morris had Rud and six children standing by to testify against the couple. But early on, she experienced a minor setback when Rud, who claimed he had attended parties with the Bentzes at which children had been molested during a game of hide-and-seek, was unable to identify Bob Bentz in court. Then an eleven-year-old boy testified that both the Bentzes had abused him sexually during two summers, but admitted on the stand the following day that he had lied in some of his testimony. The hardest part for the Bentzes came when one of their children took the stand to testify. "I felt so sorry for him," says Lois. "I knew he was lying, but I couldn't figure out how they made him do it at the time. It was really so tragic. I wanted to run up and hug him and tell him that everything was gonna be okay."

Later their son would tell them that if he had known that the boy who had testified earlier had admitted lying and nothing had happened to him, he would have admitted that he was lying too. "But I was afraid of what they would do to me. I wanted to get out of the foster home and they told us that if we got help for our Moms and Dads they would only go to jail for twenty-eight months; otherwise they'd go to jail for thirty-five years and we'd never see them again."

The child witnesses were lodged at a local hotel, where Morris presided as head cheerleader. After the first boy testified at the trial, she had him stand up in front of all the other children. "J. did a wonderful job of testifying today," she enthused. "Let's all give him a big hand." Later Morris would receive a severe rebuke from the judge for failing to follow his instructions and keep the children apart from one another during the trial.

On September 19, after Bob and Lois had testified that they had never done any of the things they were accused of, the jury retired. There were twelve charges against each of them, any one of which could have sent them to prison for years. When the jury filed back to its seats, each finding had to be read out. Only when the Bentzes heard the final verdict of "not guilty" did they realize their ordeal was over. Almost.

Morris was furious. In tears, she told reporters, "This means we live in a society that does not believe in children. I'm sick to death of things like the presumption of innocence."

Donald and Cindy Buchan were scheduled to be tried next, in October. But during his opening arguments, prosecutor Gehl Tucker electrified the courtroom by announcing that all twenty-six charges against the couple were being dropped. An even bigger bombshell came on the heels of this revelation: charges against all the remaining adults would also be dropped, said a statement issued from Morris's office, because it had become "increasingly clear that many of the children would be unable to testify in any further criminal proceedings without great emotional distress or trauma." Morris intimated that something even bigger was in the works, although she was not at liberty at that point to elaborate, since it all had "a bearing on an active criminal investigation of great magnitude."

What could possibly be bigger in this crusader's mind than child sex abuse? The answer was murder. Like Doris Bell, Morris had uncovered, after months of interrogation, allegations that children were being murdered and dismembered. Under pressure and over time, the Jordan children were telling stories of homicides they claimed to have witnessed, of babies being killed, of a black child being stabbed, and of babies being tossed into the river — after which children were forced to drink their blood.

This time the FBI moved in to investigate the charges. As the weeks went by and the investigators repeatedly failed to find evidence corroborating the new allegations, Morris's office semed to run out of revelations to disclose to a gullible public. One of the Bureau's first interview subjects was a twelve-year-old boy who had provided the most graphic details of homicides to earlier investigators. He described in detail seven occasions on which he personally had watched a child being stabbed, mutilated, and/or shot during the spring and summer of 1983. He further indicated that at least fourteen of the adults on trial and eleven children observed one child being mutilated and killed.

It was his attention to detail that riveted the investigators. He described how a caravan of cars had gone to a nearby campground one summer evening. It was so dark, he said, that one boy, while walking across the bridge that led to the campground, stumbled and fell into the water. He was rescued, but many of the children who were murdered were disposed of in the river. The whole story lost credibility, however, when it was discovered that at the time of these alleged slayings, the river had been flooding and had swept away the walkway bridge. When confronted with the inconsistencies in his story, the boy finally broke down, began crying, and admitted that he had made the stories up because "[he didn't] want to go home."

A second boy stated that he had told the earlier investigators about a number of children being ritually tortured and mutilated after witnessing a program on TV. He confessed that he had lied "because [he] wanted to please the investigators." But by far the most interesting, detailed, and significant series of disclosures had come from a twelve-year-old female who had in fact been sexually abused by James Rud, the original accused molester. She had been the first child to speak of the murder and mutilation of children. Her account was the most graphic and chilling. She had been interviewed over twenty-three times; each time her story became more bizarre and elaborate. She stated that she had seen a person stick a wine glass into the vagina of a baby girl, then stab the baby in the chest and bury it. She described young boys and men who were "forced" to have sex with her and then killed. Later she would speak of a baby being killed after having its head partly cut off. Unlike the other children, she refused to retract her statements, although she changed her story on numerous occasions. Many of the children she identified as being killed were in fact alive. By this time, one of the original investigators had observed, "[I] ... did not know what to make of her stories anymore. . . . She seems so different to me now, different than she was before." The FBI investigators finally decided that the stories were simply not believable.

Shortly thereafter, Rud, the man who had started it all when he implicated the others, was sentenced to forty years in prison.

On February 15, 1985, Hubert H. Humphrey III, Minnesota's attorney general, issued a twenty-nine-page report that left very little doubt about the quality of the investigations that had turned Jordan's sleepy rural life into a waking nightmare.

The report begins by explaining that elsewhere in the state an increasing number of child molesters had been successfully prosecuted while a judicious balance was maintained between the interests of children and the rights of accused persons. "In the Scott County cases, however," it continues, "something clearly went awry."

> The central problem with which the state and federal investigators were confronted when conducting their investigation was that many of the children had been questioned about sex abuse a large number of times. A therapist's report in February 1984 notes one child who

had already been interviewed at least thirty and possibly as many as fifty times by law enforcement or Scott County authorities. A number of other children were also repeatedly interviewed.

Repeated interviewing and discussions about abuse undermine the credibility of witnesses. [This type of procedure] can cause confusion in both adults and children. With children it raises the additional concern of suggestibility. According to some experts, children may interpret repeated interviews as demands for more or different information than they have already given. . . .

In some instances, over a period of time, the allegations of sexual abuse turned to stories of mutilations, and eventually homicide.

In addition to the problems of repeated interviewing and lack of reports, another concern [that] undermined the credibility of witnesses in these cases is "cross-germination." In some instances witnesses were told what other witnesses had stated. Sometimes two children would be interviewed together. . . .

Corroborating evidence is evidence [that] confirms the verbal allegations for a crime victim. While corroboration is rarely an absolute legal requirement in a criminal case, it is always of utmost importance. In the absence of corroboration, a criminal case boils down to a debate between the accuser and the accused. . . .

Corroborating evidence is particularly critical to both the accuser and the accused in child sex abuse cases. In the interests of the accuser, corroboration is of immeasurable value to the credibility of a victim who may be impeached due to youth, or limited memory, or limited ability to communicate. In the interest of the accused, the search for corroboration protects individuals against unjust prosecution. . . .

In spite of intensive effort of state and federal investi-

gators, no evidence was uncovered [that] would corroborate the initial allegations of the children.[6]

This model report should be posted on a prominent wall
near each judge, lawyer, police officer, social worker, and
other individual involved in these strange child-abuse trials.
It emphasizes that these lurid tales can be triggered by
repeated interviews and that the fabrication of such tales is
not necessarily brought about consciously or with malicious
intent on the part of the child or the investigating authorities.
It also brings into focus the dangers inherent in circumvent-
ing careful judicial practice.

The report concludes with recommendations and a suggestion that the Scott County experience represents a vivid
reminder "that in a just and democratic society, those in
positions of public power must bring reason and good judgment to their discretion in the exercise of power."

"In a hysterical climate," the report concludes, "society
needs to understand how to deal with community trauma."

These cases have been chosen because they are typical of the
false accusations — often involving obscene rites and murder
— that are overwhelming the courtrooms of North America.
To a large extent, these false allegations of child abuse result
from mistakes that can be put down to overzealous public
officials responding in panic to intimations of such taboo
activities as incest and child sexual abuse. Often, such allegations represent the deliberate machinations of a parent maliciously accusing an estranged spouse of molesting their
child. But the biggest puzzle for professionals and others
attempting to understand this strange new phenomenon
involves children's ability to tell these grotesque tales, which,
as Hamilton foster mother Jane Wyatt put it, "are about
things as perverse as anything that [we've] ever heard . . . and
some that [we haven't]."

More than "community trauma," society has to learn to

deal with the rights and the psychology of children. Can a child reasonably be expected to stand up in court and "tell the truth, the whole truth, and nothing but the truth?" Can a child even understand such a concept? Many would answer these questions in the negative. Children's tenuous grasp of reality, their limited knowledge base, and their chillingly demonstrated ability to embellish a lurid sexual tale with scenes that would make Manson and his breed of mass murderers pale in comparison make it difficult to deal with them in the courts.

As Ralph Underwager has suggested, and as the above cases show, there is a definite pattern to these allegations. Children start out talking about someone touching them and then move on to describe fondling and penetration. Only subsequently do their stories incorporate drug use, monsters, or witches. Often they introduce an element involving flight to and from strange places. If pressured to continue, they next bring in rainbow-colored snakes or animals trained to defecate or urinate in the children's mouths. Moving on, they describe ritual killings of small animals (usually gerbils), then of larger animals, and finally the torture, murder, and mutilation of little children. In reciting these stories, the children provide a wealth of convincing detail. Such stories at first seem utterly believable for two reasons.

First, we presume that children could not arrive at this knowledge without prior experience. This is what baffled the Hamilton investigators and led them to conclude that the young girls were speaking about experiences they had actually suffered, although Judge Beckett balked at accepting the more lurid allegations as fact. Second, such things do, in a rare few instances, actually happen. Children are beaten, sexually assaulted, and ritually sacrificed. The difference between gruesome fact and childhood fantasy is material evidence. And in our efforts to protect every child from the faintest hint of such brutal betrayal, we may unintentionally dismiss the only thing that separates the world as it is from the world that exists in the mind of a child. When these horrid experiences do actually happen to children, material evidence usually exists and plays the crucial role in determining the innocence or guilt of their accused abusers.

In February 1984, a little Florida boy named Scotty Goldman woke up screaming. His mother tried to console him, but to no avail. His behavior had been erratic for weeks, but on this particular night he was saying things that his mother did not want to hear. "A big black man . . . at nursery . . . took my pants, and he hurt me." [7] The following day his mother took him to Jackson Hospital's Rape Treatment Center. A physician there informed her that her son had been raped. Later he would confirm that her son had gonorrhea of the throat. Scotty was able to take authorities to the nursery where the abuse had taken place and pointed to the man who had done it.

That information shocked Dade County, Florida.

The media began an investigation into the state's daycare facilities. Their investigation suggested that the potential for abuse was alarmingly widespread. However, Christopher Rundle, the recently appointed state prosecutor, admitted that in the case of two-year-old Scotty Goldman, even though the evidence of sexual abuse was clear, the law did not consider a two-year-old child competent to supply information about who did it. They would need corroborating evidence; otherwise the defence would simply demolish the child's testimony.

The investigators turned to Joseph and Laurie Braga, two of the most respected, if somewhat eccentric, child psychologists in Florida, for information concerning the sexual abuse of children. During the months that followed the rape of Scotty Goldman, Dade County would hear a lot from this husband-and-wife team. They were educators and defenders of children, and their voices were sometimes alone in breaking the silence surrounding the sexual abuse of children. They had long been speaking up on behalf of abused children, and now Dade County was a little more willing to listen. Citing the statistics of abuse across the nation, the Bragas posed the painful question, "Could child molesting happen in Dade County's daycare facilities?"

Apparently it could. Midway through 1984, following an intensive media campaign to educate the public, a daycare operator named Frank Fuster was charged with sexual abuse of children. His seventeen-year-old wife, Iliana Fuster, was later charged as well. The charges came following the disclosure by a number of children who had been in the Fusters' care that the couple had routinely danced naked with them, fondled them, engaged in sodomy and mutual fellatio, drugged them, and chopped the heads off birds in what appeared to be a sacrificial ritual. Taken together, these made quite a list of violations against the children placed in their care. In the course of the ensuing investigation, it was discovered that Frank Fuster, the owner/operator of the daycare center, was a convicted child molester and murderer. This discovery, among others, enraged the parents of Dade County. Laurie and Joseph Braga explained that this was possible because of the lax security and licensing system governing daycare facilities in Florida, a point they had been arguing long before child abuse became a hot political issue.

Frank Fuster, detained in Dade County jail, protested his and his wife's innocence. This was a difficult position to maintain, given that his own son, who was said by other children to have been regularly assaulted by his father and mother, had gonorrhea of the throat.

With the prior record of the accused, and the crowd of child witnesses, the case seemed open and shut. But it wasn't. The Dade County parents who wanted a conviction had to wade painfully through the adversarial court system, reliving their children's traumas with every question in examination and cross-examination. But in their minds they had no choice.

It took over a year and a half before they secured a conviction, but during that time they successfully lobbied for changes in child-welfare legislation and brought the best minds of both schools of thought on child abuse into the legal equivalent of an OK Corral.

Previously, in order to obtain a conviction, children were forced by law to testify in the courtrooms, to confront the accused. Ever since the child-abuse "epidemic" began, this practice has been a serious point of contention for both sides. Children are easily intimidated, forced to relive the alleged trauma that had brought them into contact with the system in the first place, and generally violated once again by the very process that was meant to serve them. Joseph Braga argued that children should be allowed to be questioned in a psychologically gentler setting, one more in keeping with their age. He successfully won a motion to have the children videotaped while disclosing their stories to trained child sexual abuse experts — in this case, the Bragas. The room in which the interviews were conducted was filled with child-sized toys and furniture, and children were spoken to according to their level of development. The videotape ruling would satisfy the rule of justice that says that the accuser must face his accused, while at same time solving the problem that occurred in many cases, where the perpetrator of crimes against children has cowed them into silence by stating things like, "If you talk, terrible things will happen to you. If you talk your mothers and fathers will die." Braga had argued that a child in conventional court might not be able to overcome his or her fears, and inspired by the argument of this child-rights activist, the parents of Dade County collected a petition urging parents and politicians to follow his advice. Both the courts and the 1985 session of the Florida legislative assembly accepted his recommendations.

The legislation modifying the requirement for a face-to-face challenging in court between victim and accused had an unintended effect, however. While such laws make it easier to prosecute actual molesters or cults perpetrating atrocities on innocent children, they also make it easier for overzealous investigators to prosecute the innocent.

But in this particular case, child sexual abuse had in fact occurred, and the Fuster boy's gonorrhea of the throat proved to be the most damning piece of evidence. Taken together, the full spectrum of evidence implicated Frank Fuster and his wife, Iliana. But here the final decision, unlike the Jordan case, was based on corroborative evidence.

In his testimony before the courts, Joseph Braga argued his points on the basis of child development. He was aware that sexual abuse was uncomfortable to talk about and involved complex issues; however, he made it clear that he was on the side of the child in these cases, because someone had to be. Like others of this school, he believed that children don't lie about sexual abuse, but simply have a difficult time talking about it. He agreed, then, with Dr. Roland Summit, who was called to the stand to testify on the children-don't-lie theory. Together they underscored their side of the story — or rather the child's side as they understood it.

Many people wanted the Bragas to be right because, if the children were deemed incompetent to testify, men like Fuster (and who knew, they would argue, how many hundreds of other molesters) would be free to continue violating children's bodies. And in this case, a landmark for those who believe that children don't lie about abuse, the Bragas were right. Fuster was pronounced guilty on the basis of undeniable evidence, and the trauma of the children was reduced through the Bragas' sensitive intervention. This case showed that both sides of the child-care field have poignant stories to tell about our children, and that both must co-operate in a necessarily adversarial system of justice. The rights of the accused and the accuser must be protected. But the balance of sympathy, science, and justice has not yet been struck. And if the "experts" on whom the courts rely disagree concerning how to achieve that balance, what are the courts or the public to do?

"People generally do not understand," says Underwager, "how tremendously concerned children are with sexuality. They have strong sexual feelings — 'polymorphous perverse pleasure,' as Freud put it. Children rely on adults to keep them in touch with reality, even sexual reality as we define it for them. But in this kind of panic situation, all the authority figures — ... the therapists, police, and prosecutors — are accepting the the children's fantasies at face value." Underwager argues convincingly that if children experience this process long enough, they can become psychotic. They can certainly end up believing that abuse happened when in fact it didn't.[8]

Children are easily swayed by both the conscious and unconscious intentions and values of the adults around them. They "absorb" our fears and ideals without our consciously instructing them. Thus we can "program" them with varying degrees of success, though not always to their advantage or our own.

As will be argued at length in Chapter 5, violence — especially sexual violence — is increasing at an alarming rate. The combined threats of nuclear war, ecological devastation, and international terrorism, along with the increasingly alienating aspects of modern life, are creating a few people who are psychologically excited by violence and sex. These are the real child abusers, and though their actual number remains small, it is undeniably growing. And as the media feeds middle-class North America's fears with regular accounts of this kind of person, the general public, inundated with information from supposed experts, leans further toward accepting without question the unbelievably horrid things that our children are saying about the world around them. Quite literally, children are mirroring our world back to us in the courtrooms.

But in our desire to understand and accomodate children, we have lost sight of two crucial matters: first, how children's minds differ from those of adults; and second, the fundamental rules of justice. Had we kept these in mind, we would have noted what is obvious to observant psychologists: the lack of correspondence between the fantasies children construct and the reality around them. The principle of the presumed innocence of an accused individual unless the weight of material evidence proves otherwise forms the cornerstone of our judicial system. If we abandon it, we risk falling into an inquisitional pattern: suspicion, accusation, interrogation, and trial.

The ramifications are dangerous and confusing. And it is here, in the crucible of uncertain relationships between individual and state, between child and adult, between men and women that children have come to utter their indictments of the world around them.

3
THE NORTH AMERICAN
EXPERIENCE:
Path of an Epidemic

The zeal of the well-meaning people who are so understandably devoted to fighting the scourge that is child abuse must be scrutinized by a protection agency and courts. This zeal has created a subtle dynamic that can somehow convert a suspicion of child abuse into a presumption of child abuse. . . . This must be quite frightening to the citizens of a free and democratic society.
His Honour Judge Peter Nasmith, Toronto, 1986

The multi-billion-dollar child-care industry has spawned two diametrically opposed armies: one contending that children are being sexually assaulted and murdered at an increasingly alarming rate in unimaginably grotesque ways, and that we are only now beginning to fathom the gravity of the problem; the other asserting that this is not the case, that statistics are being misused to accomplish other political goals. Each group is equally convinced of the righteousness of its position and can marshal alleged victims and volumes of facts that fit its view.

In the middle ground, a less militant group accepts that a significant number of children are sufficiently endangered to require widespread concerned action. They believe that the children speak the truth some of the time and that in the heat of battle our task should be to attempt to distinguish between the children's statements of fact and those of fantasy and, where possible, to lend a healing hand.

These opposing groups have not always been with us. They originated about a century ago and only over the last decade have they become powerful enough to make their claims heard. Child advocates in the United States have traditionally been the torchbearers in this children's rights crusade.

According to John Alvin Lee, a University of Toronto sociologist, we can understand the changes in our attitudes toward children if we break down our ways of understanding them into three distinct models — or, as he terms them, paradigms. The influence of the first paradigm lasted until the beginning of the industrial age. Under this paradigm, children were seen basically as the property of their father, just as the mother, the servants, the domestic pets, and everything else that belonged to the family were under the control of the father. He could dispose of the children as he saw fit: he could sell them, put them out to work for the economic stability of the family — even, if need be, kill them.

After the Industrial Revolution, social attitudes toward children gradually shifted toward a more protective paradigm. People believed — and legislation reflected — that children should be protected somewhat from the whims of adults, from sexual knowledge, and from exploitation. During this period, laws were developed to protect children from cruel labor practices; limited legal rights policies were initiated; and society gave its fledgling child-care agencies the power to remove children from abusive situations. The state became the moral police governing both children and their protectors. Eventually the protection laws came to emphasize saving children from their parents' ignorance and exploitation, and preparing them for entry into the life of society. Parents, in a very real sense, were holding their children in a kind of trusteeship for the state. The effects of this philsophy can still be seen in the present: for example, special governmental permission is necessary for keeping children at home rather than sending them to school. The state demands certain actions from the parents until their child reaches the age of majority — that is, the age at which an individual is independently responsible to the state and can be rewarded or punished on his or her own merits.

From our vantage point in the late twentieth century, this may appear to be an unusual way of thinking about children and the role of their parents; however, it seems to best explain the role of the state concerning present-day charges of sexual abuse and the response of public officials to these charges. In both Canada and the U.S., if someone in authority (say, a doctor, teacher, or police officer) reports a parent for child abuse, then some officer of the state (for example, an agency like the Children's Aid Society in Canada) will apply to another instrument of the state, the courts, for permission to take the child away from the allegedly offending parent. Parents have no legal recourse in these matters but to proceed through the courts in an attempt to establish their guilt or innocence. It would almost seem as if the state has been offended.

More recently, a shift has been observable from the protective paradigm to what Lee calls the "personal paradigm of childhood," which involves looking at children as persons in their own right. From this perspective, children are viewed and treated in the same manner as women, blacks, and natives, who participate in and are rightfully entitled to the freedoms and equality guaranteed to Americans in their U.S. Constitution and to Canadians in their Charter of Rights and Freedoms.

This is still new ground for both parents and law-makers, but this is the paradigm now holding sway in North American courts. And because of its novelty and our uncertainties, significant problems are arising from it. Under the most extreme form of this evolving paradigm, children are given the rights of free persons. It is a philosophy of liberation, and as with all such philosophies — whether applied to blacks, to women, or to children — it presupposes a radical breaking of the chains that formerly held a group back. We tend under this paradigm to look at children as little adults and assume therefore that in most cases they would speak using the same concepts and cognitive structures as adults. In the cases at hand, this assumes that they would speak "the whole truth" if given half a chance. Where we have perceived severe and repeated child abuse, we have held that they needed more than "half a chance" — and have virtually instructed them in what they should say on their behalf.

The first major change in the North American social consciousness toward children was realized back in the 1870s, the heyday of the influential post–Civil War thinkers known as the Radical Reconstruction reformers, whose rhetoric on the "natural rights of man" gained popularity among the increasing number of bourgeois families who could afford to follow such noble sentiments. These enlightened ideas eventually filtered down to society's views about children. If the young could be taught the new ways of being in the world, a world unimpeded by political and religious oppression, then the world, or at least particular nations, would benefit. The idea of children having at least some basic rights became part of this rhetoric and inspired the formation of a like-minded group of child protectors. Their cause célèbre would come in the person of Mary Ellen Case, the illegitimate daughter of Francis Case.[1]

In 1874 a neighbor observed that Mary Connolly — Francis Case's second wife and Mary Ellen's stepmother — "often beat the child, and sent her out in harsh weather with scanty bits of clothing." This was brought to the attention of Henry Bergh, the founder of the American Society for the Prevention of Cruelty to Animals (ASPCA). Surely, Bergh argued, a child needs protection from the cruelty of its care-takers as much as an animal does. His eloquent arguments for Mary Ellen's removal from her home won him a place in the hearts of charitable New Yorkers.

Shortly thereafter, the first child-protection agency in North America opened: the New York Society for the Prevention of Cruelty to Children. Groups in Boston, Philadelphia, and Chicago sprang up in quick succession. They lobbied successfully for national funds, law reforms, and the right to remove children from their guardians at the agencies' discretion. By the beginning of this century these societies had in their care over 15,000 young persons (mostly in institutions, some in foster homes) and a $1.5-million budget.

Like many other individuals and organizations, however, they lost a great deal of their support during the Great Depression of the 1930s. By the end of the Second World War, money and interest had all but run out, and only a skeleton crew of government-funded agencies were left to work on behalf of children and their families. At the time, physical abuse was not the primary concern regarding child welfare: the remaining agents' British-influenced mandate called for service to "neglected children — the victims of parents who willfully or unwittingly have endangered their health, morals, welfare, or emotional development."[2] No mention was made of either the physical or sexual abuse of children.

The ideals of these pioneer child advocates were fully developed by 1959 and expressed to the world through the United Nations' Declaration of the Rights of the Child: Principle 2, which states that

> the child shall enjoy protection, and shall be given opportunities and facilities, by law and by other means, to enable him to develop physically, mentally, morally, spiritually, and socially in a healthy and normal environment and in conditions of freedom and dignity. In the enactment of laws for this purpose, the best interests of the child shall be the paramount consideration.

Principle 6 opts for a less utopian, but still lofty, ideal:

> The child, for the full and harmonious development of

his personality, needs love and understanding. He shall, wherever possible, grow up in the care and under the responsibility of his parents, and, in any case, in an atmosphere of affection and of moral and material secu-rity.

The poor funding allocated to the North American social agencies of the late 1950s, combined with a general popula-tion that was indifferent to their cause, resulted in a more prosaic social reality. But three years after this international proclamation — and nearly two decades after America's national child-welfare system had virtually run its course — public interest and federal dollars began to work once again on behalf of the nation's children.

The new impetus came from pediatricians — who had long known about, but done little to help, the battered chil-dren who frequently appeared in their examination rooms. As a group, pediatricians had been reluctant to label the many children they saw with broken bones, contusions, and other "accidental" injuries as victims of child abuse.

That changed dramatically when, in 1962, the *Journal of the American Medical Association* published a landmark child-abuse study.[3] Pediatricians C. Henry Kempe and F. N. Silver-man, in their article "The Battered Child Syndrome," anticipated with remarkable clarity the issues that remain prevalent among child and family-service advocates today: Who are these parents and why do they do such things to their children? Are adult abusers villains or victims? Should the state intervene? If so, at what point, and to what extent? How extensive is the problem? While unable to state precisely the magnitude of the problem, Kempe conveyed powerfully the deep sense of urgency that he felt was needed in responding to the issue. In his conclusion, he writes:

> Psychiatric factors are probably of prime importance in the pathogenesis of the disorder, but our knowledge of these factors is limited. Parents who inflict abuse on

their children do not necessarily have psychopathic or sociopathic personalities or come from borderline socioeconomic groups, although most published cases have been in these categories. In most cases some defect of character structure is probably present; often parents may be repeating the type of child care practiced on them.

Kempe and Silverman's cogent, insightful article acted as a call to arms from one of the most powerful and prestigious groups in America. And it identified the problem as one belonging to all social classes. Because of this, it received immediate widespread attention.

The national media took up the cause through editorials and an increased number of reports on issues surrounding child abuse. Their response galvanized public support. The government itself responded with limited funding. Scholars began to study abuse from all sides — medical/psychiatric, socioeconomic, criminological — and widely disseminated their studies in a number of interdisciplinary journals: journals of medicine, law, government, society, biological and behavioral medicine, and psychiatry — and at least two journals devoted specifically to child abuse and neglect.

In little more than a decade, these newly recognized interests were organized into a cohesive instrument capable, it was hoped, of controlling what was gradually being perceived as a massive social problem.

In 1974 the U.S. government introduced a comprehensive *Child Abuse Prevention and Treatment Act,* which established a program of federal grants to states that met specified eligibility requirements. At the time only three states satisfied those requirements, but less than a decade later all but four states had passed new child-protection laws enabling them to qualify for this new source of federal aid.[4]

The creation of the National Center for Child Abuse and Neglect in 1974 spearheaded the development of rapid state-by-state uniformity of child-protection laws. The National

Center was responsible for gathering and disseminating information on a nationwide basis. It co-ordinated efforts to increase the reporting of child abuse, and specifically that of physical and sexual abuse. This marked the first official federal government response to child sexual abuse, an issue that had not even existed up to that time as far as social service policy was concerned. By the middle 1980s, statistics would indicate that the problem had reached epidemic proportions. While child-abuse statistics vary, the following table suggests the effects of these new reporting laws:[5]

Year	Estimated number of child victims of sexual abuse	Rate per 10,000 children
1976	7,559	1.14
1977	11,617	1.77
1978	12,257	1.89
1979	27,247	4.25
1980	37,366	5.87
1981	37,441	5.93
1982	56,607	9.02
1983	71,961	11.50

Such figures led many to conclude that child sexual abuse was increasing. Others argued that abuse had always been with us, but only now were we beginning to acknowledge it. One of the primary groups focusing attention on the problem were the early feminists, whose concern over the apparently mounting incidence of rape had led to the establishment of rape-crisis centers during the late 1960s and early 1970s. Rape had hitherto been regarded as the most pernicious manifestation of male aggression toward those less powerful. But as time went on and women found the courage to talk to one another about things they had always kept hidden, it emerged that incest was an even darker shared secret.

It was during this period that the confessional books about incest began to appear — books with titles like *Kiss Daddy Goodnight* and *Daddy's Girl*. Pornography too was becoming an issue, especially child pornography. Fuelled by books like Andrea Dworkin's furious polemic, *Pornography: Men Possessing Women*, the outrage against male domination spilled over into the general female population. One no longer had to be a militant feminist to understand what was happening. Child abuse had become everyone's concern. This was brought about by the gradual change in social attitudes toward children, attitudes that might be characterized by our collective answers to the questions "To whom do children belong?" "What are their inherent rights?"

It should not be surprising that women are on the leading edge of the revolutionary changes in our attitudes toward children. Adult women and young girls, after all, are the most commonly victimized. Through this issue feminists neatly brought together several major concerns regarding male/female relations — rape, incest, and pornography — issues that remain at the heart of the child-abuse puzzle today.

But if it appeared clear to many that child sex abuse was increasing, it was less clear just how prevalent it was or what kind of action should be taken. The National Center for Child Abuse and Neglect had the difficult job of collecting unbiased data — a job vastly complicated by the number of emotionally involved groups with vested interests. By 1978, concern about child abuse had given rise to a multi-billion-dollar industry in the United States, employing tens of thousands of diversely motivated professionals. In the minds of a hysterical public, however, the criteria for assessing abuse remained informal and continue to vary widely. The problem of adequately defining abuse still confounds the social agencies concerned.

A child does not have to be physically beaten or sexually molested to be considered abused. Nor does the child need to be grossly neglected. In the ambiguous world of child-abuse laws, loose terminology plays an increasingly problematic role. Consider again the term "abused child." This immediately brings to mind children who are beaten, sexually assaulted, consistently undernourished, and sickly as a result of parental neglect. When we hear reports from government agencies or child-abuse investigators of more than a million children being "abused" each year, these are the children that come most readily to mind. But we do not yet really know what percentage of children are maltreated to the point that their mental or physical well-being, in the short or long term, is endangered. The majority of cases that are consuming our time and resources involve children who can be loosely described as emotionally deprived, inadequately loved, educationally neglected — that is, as being in serious, perhaps, but not life-threatening, situations. Given the varying statistics, the lumping together of reliable and unfounded reports, and vagaries of definition, it is difficult to get a true picture of how many children of these "million each year" are actually in significant danger.

A second area of ambiguity can be seen in the diverse standards that define abuse. For example, the state of New Jersey defines emotional abuse as "inadequate love." What is adequate? Whose standards should be applied here?

In addition to the problems with defining abuse and deciding what kinds of adult behavior constitute abuse, there is a reporting problem. In order to identify endangered children, the law requires all medical, educational, social work, child-care, and law enforcement professionals to report suspected cases, and imposes civil and criminal penalties on those who fail to do so. These professionals, not wanting to expose themselves to such reprisals, report a large number of marginal cases based on loosely defined ideas of what constitutes child abuse. Most state laws also include provisions that encourage relatives, neighbors, and friends of a family to report suspected maltreatment. In fact, in nineteen states "any person [read "any absolute stranger"] who has reason to suspect child abuse or neglect" is *required* to report it.[6] This has led to an overwhelming number of unsubstantiated or unfounded charges.

Public-awareness campaigns, combined with clumsy definitions and mandatory reporting, have been strikingly effective in increasing the number of reports of child abuse. For example, in 1963, the year after Kempe and Silverman's article came out, approximately 150,000 youths considered to be victims of child abuse came to the attention of U.S. public authorities. Ten years later that figure had risen to nearly 600,000. By 1985, over 1.9 million children were reported abused. Federal aid to child-protection programs in 1962 equalled approximately $138,000. By 1974 it had risen to $3.7 million a year, while today state and federal expenditures for such programs exceed $3.9 billion.[7] At the same time an entire industry of "experts" — consisting of psychologists, community workers, lawyers, and others — has been created to deal with the problem.

Does this mean that there has been an actual increase in child abuse or neglect? This is a difficult question to answer. Some people think that a real rise has occurred since 1972, and attribute it to deteriorating economic and social conditions. They argue that the successfully implemented educational programs, media support, and mandatory reporting laws have led to much more accurate reporting of the incidence of child abuse. The corresponding belief that this type of violence also reflects years of child abuse in the histories of its perpetrators profoundly influences public reaction to the problem.

But statistics do not show the number of unfounded reports. Indiscriminately mixed with valid reports, they provide a false total. For instance, in New York State, the Department of Social Services received 75,000 child-abuse reports in 1983, an increase of nearly 50 per cent since 1979. But approximately 20 per cent of these reports were unsubstantiated. This means that in New York alone, 23,000 innocent families were investigated. The National Center of Child Abuse and Neglect estimates that a full 60 per cent of all reports of suspected child maltreatment turn out to be unfounded, after a child-protection agency does an investigation.[8] This means that more than 750,000 families nationwide are needlessly investigated. The much publicized increase in the incidence of abuse, then, could be based on unfounded reports, on more sophisticated and uniform reporting laws and records of such reports, or — and least likely — an actual higher number of sexually abused children.

In order to accomplish the laudable goal of intervening productively into the lives of abused children, we need more realistic and graded definitions of child abuse. When we hear that there are more than one million maltreated children, it should be made clear that this figure does not refer to substantiated cases of gross sexual abuse, or brutally battered children. Of this number, only approximately 6 per cent are abused to the point that they require medical care, and only 7 per cent are sexually abused.[9] As desirable as it may be to help all children who are "emotionally neglected," "inadequately nurtured," or "deprived of affection," we may well ask whether or not we want state institutions to provide for these needs. Recognizing that all these admittedly serious, but certainly not life-threatening, problems are included under the term "child abuse" would go a long way toward reducing the mounting public hysteria and placing the child-care industry on a course that is at once positive and realistic. In time, perhaps, we can reorder social life, and especially male aggression; but for now, it must be enough to do a less ambitious task reasonably and well rather than do an overwhelming one unreasonably and poorly.

But the bare statistics are what the public and the government agencies hear about. The response of the public — and ultimately of the state — is to call for even more stringent laws and recommend spending even more money to alleviate the problem. For instance, in New York in 1984, over 40 new child-abuse bills were introduced; California passed 50 new bills in the same year.[10] Despite the enormous public spending and widespread concern, the sprawling child-care-industry battalions are neither sufficiently organized nor sufficiently aware of how to deal with the vast majority of children and families who come into the state's care.

Consider some of the ways in which an unfounded report arises. For the most part it will reflect only the best of intentions. A school teacher is educated by the local child-abuse awareness programs and is prompted by both her sympathy and the mandatory reporting laws, to file a report. She notes that a particular child comes to school in dirty clothes every day and the legal and moral question she asks herself is whether or not this child has been abused. Often she will err on the side of caution, as many people do, both for her own sake and for the child's. Another child may have a suspicious-looking bruise, and whether or not there is evidence of parental assault he too is reported as abused.

Until recently, most child sex abuse was discovered when a child spontaneously told someone about it. With the stronger reporting laws, media hype, and education, we are now seeing situations in which the abuse allegations surface when an adult begins to question a child. This is becoming more and more common in child-custody disputes, but such accusations are increasing against teachers, babysitters, daycare workers, and others involved in the care of youngsters.

Certainly, not all cases of abuse turn out to be unfounded, but given the uncertainties and hyperawareness of possible abuse, many behaviors are labelled abusive when in fact they are not. In Minnesota, for instance, a nine-year-old boy was discovered "playing suggestively" with his seven-year-old sister. At another time this might have been seen as part of children's natural exploration, a way of coming to understand their budding sexuality. But in 1983 this child was taken to court, removed from his home, and placed on probation for three years. This case is not particularly unusual any more; it illustrates the questionable labelling of abuse, and thus may help to explain the increase of abuse reports.

False accusations, while obvious infringements of the rights accused individuals, also create a further problem: an overloading of the already strained family service system. When this happens, it becomes even more difficult to deal effectively with children and families who truly need atten-tion. Forced to allocate a substantial portion of their resources to following up on unfounded reports, these agen-cies are increasingly unable to respond promptly and effec-tively when children are in serious danger.

Decision-making among child-abuse investigators suffers as a result of their staggering caseload. Workers "burn out" or become desensitized to the real warning signals of imminent danger to a child. Burnout of professionals in the child-abuse investigation area is an increasingly common phenomenon. Workers are, of course, often overworked, underpaid, unde-rappreciated, and criticized — some of the more obvious reasons that they burn out. But in terms of child protection, which is what their mandate is all about, the real problem is that people who are only half-committed to their work will be unable to respond effectively on behalf of those who truly need their assistance. Turnover within child-welfare institu-tions will remain high, forcing management to channel a disproportionate amount of funds into staff training. In prac-tical terms this means that those who are investigating child abuse or neglect will be less capable of carrying out effective investigations because they will be less experienced in deal-ing with real, imagined, or borderline abuse cases, and inca-pable of discerning among the three. It takes years of experience for a social worker to learn to deal effectively with the dynamics of a family with serious problems. And the weight of the decisions to intervene into the life of a family by removing the victim and/or by otherwise treating the offender is simply too profound a responsibility to be left in the hands of undertrained or burnt-out caseworkers.

It is reported that between 35 and 55 per cent of all child-abuse fatalities and tens of thousands of injuries involve children who have been previously known to the child- and family-welfare authorities.[11] Their front-line workers' knowledge of the family and the law is crucial, since they will launch the investigation and pull together the team of resource people who will determine if abuse has in fact occurred. But to determine this requires an intensive investigation that is unavoidably traumatic and inherently a breach of parental and family privacy. Indeed, with the laws as they are in many states, complete strangers can initiate this type of investigation against a family.

To determine if the child is in danger, caseworkers must inquire into the intimate details of a family's life. Quite often the workers must question friends, relatives, and neighbors, as well as schoolteachers, daycare personnel, physicians, and clergy who know the family. Both the scope and the emotional intensity of this background investigation are extremely exhausting.

A significant contributor to the increasing numbers of unfounded reports is the "abuse hotline." This is becoming a major public reporting avenue in many states. In most cases callers are permitted to remain anonymous, and workers in half the states are counselled to screen out only "inappropriate" reports. Malicious people and an uninformed general public caught up in a crippling, hysterical climate, are given an easy place to vent their claims. One writer found that a child-abuse investigation was initiated on the basis of a caller reporting that a seventeen-year-old boy was found "in a drunken stupor." Perhaps that boy's family might benefit from counselling, but to start a full-fledged investigation based on this information is simply not warranted.

If one multiplies such cases by the thousands and projects them across the United States, one gets some sense of the problem. Child advocates are loudly proclaiming the need for more staff, more research, more resources to handle the mounting number of abused children. But when they are forced to spend much of their time on these marginal cases, the agencies are finding themselves unable to respond to children who are in truly neglectful or dangerous environments.

Of course this is not a problem area that child-welfare officials are willing to discuss in public. It would lessen their credibility, and more importantly their ability to deal with those families who are seriously in need of the state's special services. This concern has been outlined by Douglas Besherov, the former director of the U.S. National Center for Child Abuse and Neglect who resigned in the face of the mounting number of false accusations brought about by the current legislation — legislation that he himself had spearheaded with the best of intentions. And as the public realizes that hundreds of thousands of innocent people are being victimized while many truly endangered children are going unprotected, a backlash of public opinion will surely develop to erode continued support for child-protection efforts at the federal and the state government levels.

Nobody wants this to happen. For despite the cogent criticisms levelled against social agencies, the all-too-real problems of child abuse require an efficient, caring, knowledgeable, and widespread network of organizations.

There is another disturbing consequence of the exaggerated figures reported daily in the national media, the statistics that unnecessarily exacerbate existing public hysteria, generating even more reports and therefore more hysteria. Teachers, daycare workers, estranged spouses, and others affected by this wave of accusations talk about refraining from contact with children. No hugs, no pats on the back, no touching of any kind. The consequences are simply too dangerous. This is especially ironic for those men who have spent the last decade listening to messages telling them to be sensitive, caring, and feeling as opposed to tough, distant, and macho, especially toward children.

Since the early 1970s, the struggle of U.S. child advocates to have child abuse recognized as a serious social problem requiring sustained government response has succeeded, perhaps beyond their wildest dreams. Roland Summit collected the prevailing ideas about child abuse and neglect into a coherent interventionist strategy characterized by the slogan "Children Don't Lie." Alice Miller and Florence Rush published profoundly disturbing accounts of child sexual abuse and its consequences. Their work shocked already sensitized North American and Western European audiences. For its part, Canada launched its own child-welfare reformation programs, which mirror many of the U.S. assumptions and practices.

In 1974, when the U.S. was establishing its first organized national response to the child-abuse problem, Canada was in the process of launching a major national commission. Initially set up by the government of British Columbia to study family and child law in that province, it amounted in the end to a "complete examination of child welfare throughout Canada." Presided over by the Honourable Thomas R. Berger, Chief Justice of British Columbia, the study set out the fundamental questions that would guide its own and future research into Canadian child-welfare laws.

Mr. Justice Berger believed that the fundamental issue was the question of state intervention into the lives of "dependent" people. He posed the question "When can the state take a child from its parents?" His interest in the rights of dependent people had been clearly demonstrated in his journey across northwestern Canada and into the Arctic listening to native claims and assessing their fundamental rights during the famous Alaska pipeline inquiry. When the law per-ceives people as dependent, the state usually appoints a guardian with substantial powers over their lives. Such protection, Mr. Justice Berger argued, has historically been the concern of liberal-minded reformers. Their purposes have been entirely benevolent, although their effects have not. But children are a special class of dependent, the most helpless of special-interest groups. The sacrosanct status of the nuclear family makes intervention on the behalf of children particularly delicate. Mr. Justice Berger's premise was that there are definitely children who are abused to the degree that the state should intervene and remove the children from their parents or guardians. But the question was, by whose standards are we to judge?

The Commission sought first to spell out the needs of children — such as clothing, shelter, warmth, affection, emotional security, mental health, and education — and went on to recommend that these needs should be seen as rights and legislated accordingly. They took the position that a child is entitled to some rights as a human being.

Do children in fact have a "right" to a permanent home, or to adequate services in their home, or a particular level of care and treatment? Can we presume to legislate affection? The Berger Commission's attempts to answer these fundamental questions would be modelled on the United States' example, as indicated by K. L. Levitt, a social worker and one of the leading researchers employed by the Commission. He stated:

> There are no Canadian textbooks on child welfare policy and practice, and hence schools of social work, child care, and other human services teaching units rely on U.S. publications. . . . This dependence inevitably influences what is taught, what is learned, and what becomes professional practice in Canada.[12]

Thus, despite the good intentions of this influential and far-reaching study, we are currently following in the footsteps of our U.S. social service counterparts. And their brief history suggests that this may be a serious error.

There are very few points of agreement between child-rights activists. Three fundamental issues create dissension: What is the status of children as members of the state? What are the appropriate divisions of responsibility between the state and parents in the stewardship of children? and How can parents and children be best motivated to carry out their responsibilities? The activists assume that some kind of pact exists between the state and the family, the breaking of which by any of the parties elicits a response from the other. The purpose of the Berger Commission was to analyze the assumptions of this implicit pact and to suggest which alternative was best.

In Canada many believe that however important the care of children is, it is not the proper business of the state. Parents have the primary responsibility for meeting the basic needs of their children, although health and education are concerns shared by them and the state. According to this view, the child-welfare system should intervene only when the life of the child is threatened, or the level of care is well below community standards. Child-welfare services that follow this model work to ensure child safety and provide alternative care where necessary. Needs are identified and action implemented primarily by social workers acting together with lawyers, child-care workers, police, and a limited number of medical/psychiatric practitioners.

A second view, more in keeping with the ideals of the Berger Commission, holds that children are a vulnerable group with special needs and rights. Because the state is ultimately dependent on the child — as a member of the next generation — the state is then responsible for more than the child's simple safety. Within this framework, a society's understanding of what constitute the needs of a child should be incorporated into its economic, educational, housing, health, and other social-welfare policies. This view is steadily gaining philosophical support among child advocates, and its effects were amply demonstrated in 1986 and 1987 by groups lobbying for federally funded daycare programs. They argued that it is justified and necessary for working women in present socioeconomic conditions to place their children in safe, nurturing, federally funded environments. Most social workers support this view, since it accords with the individual rights and social justice goals of their profession, and with their training in developing and implementing social programs. However, the pragmatic realities of providing for child welfare being what they are, governments until recently have for the most part responded according to the premises of the first view until recently, while researchers and child advocates have struggled with only moderate success to implement the latter.

The various statutes governing child welfare in Canada today are primarily concerned with who shall have custody and guardianship of children. They define the minimum standard of care and behavior permitted in the care of children and the process by which custody and guardianship will be changed if these minimum standards are not met. Most of these Acts are provincial responsibilities. They carry such titles as Family Relations, Adoption, Child Paternity, Family and Child Services, and Mental Health Legislation.[13]

These Acts, which provide blueprints for social service action, also crystallize the dilemma facing every child-care worker in the country and, indirectly, the dilemma of all Canadians. They reflect society's fundamental uncertainties about the responsibility of the state, the sanctity of the family, and the value of children. While in theory we care about all three, it is hoped in practice that the worker counselling the individual family will sort out the priorities and make the right decision in each case. This is an awesome responsibility. As is demonstrated by the increasing number of civil rights casualties in the U.S., the balancing act is difficult, and the wrong decisions, when made, can be very damaging.

Following Bergers' report, the federal government spon-
sored its own study to address the concerns of the public
regarding sexual abuse, and update the law as it affected
children. This resulted in the enormously influential *Report of
the Committee on Sexual Offenses Against Children* (also known as
the Badgley Report).[14] Begun in 1980, this study more than
any other to date responded to concerns of the Canadian
public and of child advocates regarding child sexual abuse. At
the time there was still very little awareness among the Canadian public, but there was enough concern among professionals to warrant the long and important study that
confirmed their growing fears.

The report was commissioned by the federal government
in 1979 and completed in 1984 — by no coincidence, the most
active years of the U.S.'s struggle against child abuse and sexual assault. The two-volume, 1,300-page document chronicles
very bluntly the kinds of brutal abuses that children routinely
suffer. Its blueprint for action comes directly out of the
research and recommendations of the U.S. National Center
for Child Abuse and Neglect. The report offers startling conclusions that fuelled the fears of the Canadian public, and the
concern at all levels of government. And those fears, in Canada as in the U.S., continue to provide a strong rationalization
for increasing the authority of social service officials.

The Badgley Report has furnished the fledgling Canadian
child-care industry with what it suggests are definitive statistics on the prevalence of child sexual abuse in Canada. As
part of its research, the report commissioned a random national survey of 2,138 individuals, 94 per cent of whom
responded to a written questionnaire. Subjects were asked
whether, at any time, "any unwanted sexual acts" had ever
been committed against them and how old they were when
these incidents occurred. Concerning sexual touching and
assault they were asked questions like the following:

Has anyone ever touched the sex parts of your body when you didn't want this?
   Never happened to me ____ or circle as many as apply of:
      touched your penis, crotch, breasts, buttocks, or anus;
      kissed/licked your penis, crotch, breasts, or anus;
      other types of touching (specify)."

Has anyone ever tried to have sex with you when you didn't want this, or sexually attacked you?
   Never happened to me ____ or circle as many as apply of:
      tried putting a penis in your vagina;
      tried putting something else (a finger or an object) in your vagina;
      tried putting a penis in your anus;
      forced a penis in your vagina;
      forced something else in your vagina;
      forced a penis in your anus;
      forced something else in your anus;
      stimulated or masturbated your crotch or penis;
      other acts (specify)."

Report results were widely interpreted as implying that by the time they are fifteen, 6 per cent of boys and 15 per cent of girls have been the subject of sexual assault that violates the Criminal Code of Canada. By seventeen years of age, 9 per cent of boys and 22 per cent of girls have been victims of sexual assault.

Among the female victims, 18 per cent of the assaults were perpetrated by a stranger, 10 per cent involved a close blood relative (sibling, parent, or grandparent); 14 per cent involved other degrees of blood relative or family members, such as step-parents; 1 per cent involved persons in a position of trust, such as a teacher; and 57 per cent involved someone else known to the victim. Females were also said to be vulnera-

ble throughout their lives to "gangs of predatory and dangerous adolescent males." The report goes on to say that only 41
per cent of the female child victims and 26 per cent of the
male victims reported the assault to anyone in authority. The
respondents cited reasons for not reporting: "It was so personal"; "I was too ashamed" or "too angry"; "thought I would
be blamed"; "didn't want to hurt my family," and so on. The
report's writers were particularly alarmed by the long-term
consequences of abuse indicated by the many confessional
letters they received, often from women who had no one to
whom they could speak about their experiences. These letters
provide an emotionally charged backdrop to the formal statistics that constitute the bulk of the report and guide its final
recommendations.

Members of the Badgley committee were shocked by their
findings, which confirmed their previously untested suspicions. They called for immediate and widespread action. In
their conclusion they wrote,

> Sexual offenses are committed so frequently and against
> so many persons that there is an evident and urgent
> need to afford victims greater protection than [what is]
> now being provided. The findings of the National Sur-
> vey clearly show the compelling nature of the fears and
> stigma associated with having been a victim of sexual
> offense. . . . What is required is the recognition by all
> Canadians that children and youth have the absolute
> right to be protected from these offenses. To achieve this
> purpose, a major shift in the fundamental values of
> Canadians and in social policies by government must be
> realized.
>
> The Committee is aware that these basic changes will
> not come about easily or quickly. If no action is taken, or
> if only token programs are initiated, the risk that chil-
> dren and youths will continue to be sexually abused will
> remain intolerably high. In this respect, one of the Com-

mittee's major recommendations is that the Office of the Commissioner [that] we recommend be established have as one of its principal responsibilities, in coopera-tion with the provinces and nongovernmental agencies, the development, co-ordination and implementation of a continuing national program of public education and health promotion focusing on the prevention of sexual offenses and the protection of young children, youths, and adults who are victims.[15]

The report also serves to support those research findings that, as explained above, demonstrate that half of the growing number of teenage drug-abusers, prostitutes (boys and girls), and other deviant adolescents have been victims of child-hood sexual assaults.

The temper and direction of the Badgley Report is summa-rized in the brief outline above; its commitment to ferret out the "street facts" and comment upon them with an emotional honesty that is rare in the archives of government commis-sions elevated its findings in the minds of its writers into a kind of child-advocate manifesto. Given their findings, it would be hard for anyone, within the government or outside it, to disagree with them. And so far nobody really has. Some feminists argue that it does not go far enough, despite its sweeping recommendations for change. But most readers are sobered by its stirring indictments regarding those it per-ceives as the victims of child abuse. Listen to its invective against pimps:

> In the Committee's judgment, the relationship between young prostitutes and pimps encompasses one of the most severe forms of abuse of children and youth, sexual or otherwise, that currently occurs in Canadian society. The relationship is based on two forms of ruthless exploitation: psychological and economic. The pimp exploits and cultivates the prostitute's vulnerabilities — her low self-esteem, her feelings of helplessness, her

loneliness on the street, and her need for love and protection. These weaknesses are the fetters with which the
pimp binds the girl to him and keeps her on the street.
Economically, pimps exploit prostitutes by drawing
them into a form of virtual slave labour, or at least into a
relationship in which one party, the pimp, provides a
service whose value is vastly outweighed by the amount
[that] the other party, the prostitute, is required to pay
for it. The cost to the prostitute of working for a pimp
goes far beyond the earnings that she gives him; it
amounts to the girl's forfeiture of her future. . . . In the
Committee's judgment, it must be viewed as a problem
of the utmost gravity. It must be stopped.[16]

The Badgley Report goes further in defining the child-
abuse issue and the appropriate Canadian response to it by
outlining a series of recommendations, the most major of
which would be to establish in Canada a national information body modelled after the National Center for Child
Abuse in the U.S.

The problem is that the Badgley Report has been *too* influential. It has not carefully concerned itself with the cluster of
individuals whose lives have been ruined not because — or at
least not exclusively because — of sexual trauma, but by poverty, ignorance, state institutions, and other misfortunes. It
did not single out those deviant personalities whose sad and
sorry condition stems from causes other than sexual assault.
It is clear that when families malfunction severely, sexuality is
only one of the areas in which their dysfunction will manifest
itself. Nor did the report mention that 23 of the last 27 violent
serial rapist-murderers arrested in the U.S. had not been sexually assaulted when young, but had been institutionalized.
Their lives had indeed been traumatic, but sexual assault is
only one of the links in the chain of dysfunction and consequent despair or deviance they displayed in later adult life.
The linking of deviance with sexuality to the exclusion of

other factors represents a narrow and inaccurate perspective. Its apparent objectivity is misleading and dangerous.

In 1987 a Parliamentary Committee consisting of seven MPs held hearings regarding Bill C-15, a bill based on the recommendations of the Badgley Report and fought for by feminists in an attempt to protect young people from sexual abuse. During its controversial passage through Parliament a group of MPs' wives from all parties stated publicly that "it is our responsibility as mothers and grandmothers to ensure that one group — children and youth — does not fall prey to another, more powerful, group". These women were express-ing what we all feel in the face of the apparent increase in violent crimes against children, crimes that have been going on for centuries with no one to champion the victims' cause.

Bill C-15 was especially supportive of changes in law that would make it easier for children to testify in court — and for their abusers to be convicted. They strongly recommended that videotapes be admissible in court; that judges be empo-wered to exclude accused people from the courtroom so the child would not feel intimidated; and (most controversial of all) that no corroboration of a child's testimony be required in order to convict an alleged abuser. The latter recommenda-tion was intended to respond to the problem of prosecuting child abusers who traditionally perpetrate their crimes in isolated places, with only themselves and their child victims present. The Committee recommendations were intended to provide children with greater protection and security.

Women who have been fighting for years for these kinds of changes have applauded Bill C-15 in most respects. On the other hand, many lawyers see significant problems arising. Bob Wakefield, president of the Canadian Association of Criminal Defense Lawyers, sees the legislation as a corrup-tion of Canada's adversarial judicial system, which depends on lawyers' being able to challenge testimony — including that of children's — to determine its truth. If we can take the

United States system as a model, this is an accurate assessment of where the problems will arise.

But through the Badgley Report and the introduction of
Bill C–15, Canadian feminists, following the example of their
U.S. counterparts, see a possibility that has been denied them
in their century-old fight for equality with men. Mary Lou
Fassel, a prominent Toronto lawyer, has argued that the Criminal Code of Canada is a bastion of dominant-male view-
points. At public meetings she has lashed out at members of
civil libertarian associations who argue vociferously against
the implementation of the changes in the rules of evidence
that Bill C–15 proposes. Their argument, she maintains "is
based upon a two-hundred-year old patriarchal legal system
[that], when it comes to sexual crimes against women, has
always favored men. It stands to protect and ultimately benefit the accused — mainly men." The fight, as Fassel under-
stands it, is not between civil libertarians and lawyers, nor
between children and adults, but between men and women.
Fassel argues that while working to change the rules of evidence for battered women and victims of rape, she and her
colleagues met the same male-dominated legal perspective
blocking the prosecution of offenders. Children's issues, she
maintains, are no different: "Women . . . are becoming silenced again [regarding the issue of child abuse]. . . . Criminal
law was never made to take account of the experience of
women. This is why the system has been unable to deal with
violence against women, whether it's violent assault as in
rape, or wife-battering, or sexual assault of children, specifically females." In her final answer to lawyers and civil libertarians who oppose the new legislation on the basis of the
fundamental rights of the accused, she strongly suggests that
"women must get fully behind these proposed changes in
evidence and . . . must tell [their opponents] that we do not
care about the rights of others if they are not the rights that
address our lives."

Traditionally, it has been impossible to get a conviction based solely on the word of a child. Accepting childrens' testimony without other evidence would, feminists feel, do away with the defence of molesters. But if children can be taught to tell a tale of abuse, as has been demonstrated in the U.S. trials, during which overzealous child advocates helped suggestible children to disclose their "secrets," what are we to make of a law that puts such emphasis on the word of these children? The debate regarding Bill C–15 is a telling commentary on the range of issues related to child abuse. It is an indirect and effective assault on the patriarchal assumptions at the heart of Canadian law.

It may be instructive to recall what was happening in America while this document was being prepared. Over 100 cases allegedly involving sex rings and satanic rituals came before the courts. Upon close investigation many of the accusations could not be substantiated. That is, despite the gravity of the charges and the determination of the prosecutors to bring to justice all people who would perpetrate such acts on innocent children, the grounds upon which investigations and eventually the trials were based in the vast majority of cases could not be proved. There was no evidence. Such sensational trials are unusual at any time, but the fact that scores of them occurred simultaneously is difficult to credit until one remembers the witch-hunts that blighted Europe throughout the fourteenth- to eighteenth- centuries.

While our abiding concern with children's welfare is totally justified, the performance of U.S. courts on behalf of American children should give us sufficient reason for entering this area cautiously. To attempt to establish a legal solution that recognizes the fundamental rights of both the accused and the accuser is what justice is all about. This suggestion is in no way meant to trivialize the incidence or consequences of actual abuse. It is simply to restate that the position taken by proponents of Bill C–15 and the Badgley Report draws the courts into the hysteria surrounding child abuse. And it is the courts, the only place where an objective finding can settle the question of innocence or guilt, that need to remain above the emotional fray.

Given the direction urged by Bill C–15, we should expect an increased number of reports of gross sexual abuse, followed by allegations of child molestation sex rings and satanic rituals, to surface in Canada. This is already happening. Hamilton hosted the first major satanic case. A second was slated to start there following the first trial. Another investigation, rumored to have links to the first Hamilton case started in London, Ontario, in late 1986. A third case, this one involving a mother accused of chanting while involving her children in ritual sexual acts, came before a family court in Toronto early in 1987. Montreal has also had a number of closed-door cases of this nature. And Vancouver, widely rumored to be the hotbed of satanic cults in this country, in early 1987 initiated a quiet investigation into the alleged ritual abuse of a young boy and girl. According to George Caldwell, the director of the Ontario Association of Children's Aid Societies, satanism has been linked to fourteen cases of child abuse during the past three years. In light of this, he is calling for a provincial inquiry into satanism and considering training child welfare workers in a knowledge of satanic practice. Despite these public statements, there has been no conclusive evidence to corroborate such charges.

Although they are beginning to speak out, by and large, Canadian child-care workers, having learned perhaps from the Hamilton case, are less conspicuous about their investigations since the public is not yet ready to believe these allegations without stable evidence. Indeed, this quieter course of action was given credence by no less a figure than Roland Summit at a 1987 Toronto conference attended by over 250 Canadian child-care workers. He correctly suggested that sensational child-abuse cases involving allegations of rituals and murders are a potential minefield for child-care workers. "It is not safe to report this kind of thing," he stated. While he personally believes that there is something real and serious behind such charges of ritual abuse, he cautioned that we do not yet understand them well enough to prosecute effectively. He advised that overly hasty action will fail to protect the children and will generate a backlash of public opinion against false accusations. Because of this, he warned, child-care workers must be careful.

The evolution of the child-abuse crisis in the United States has given rise to various kinds of problems in Canada. Day-care centers, a matter of highest priority for the growing ranks of working parents and consequently for the present government, have become a target for sexual-abuse investigators. Indeed, daycare is in a crisis right now in the United States because the increasing number of reports of gross sexual assaults said to be taking place in such centers has scared off would-be workers. If even parents are becoming cautious about touching their children, how much more cautious must daycare guardians, who are parental surrogates, become in the wake of damaging public suspicions?

As intimated, even normal parent–child relationships are being altered. For example, in Toronto in 1987, children from kindergarten to grade 6 at Regent Park area schools joined nearly 80,000 other Toronto children who have been instructed by "good touch/bad touch" programs. As part of the Prevention Education Program of the Metropolitan Toronto Special Committee on Child Abuse, a play is presented that may be generating unnecessarily widespread mistrust and alarm among children about their families. One of the central characters of this play, a jovial old uncle, arrives with a present for a little girl, saying "Don't I get a kiss?" He has already greeted her with a pinch and a tickle. The girl refuses and her mother, surprised at first, supports her. Turning to the audience, the girl asks if she should have kissed her uncle. And in chorus, all the children in the audience squirm in their chairs, giggling and saying "No, no — don't do it!"

Such programs may seem harmless enough, but the question arises, what if all uncles were perceived the same way, or if all affection were greeted with the same negative suspicion? Admittedly, given the statistics, which show that children's relatives are more likely than strangers to commit abuse against them, the intent seems justified. Childen are told that their body is their own, and they have rights and legitimate feelings, that there is a difference between touch that exploits their innocence and vulnerability and touch that is caring and affectionate. But still, the seeds of a terrible doubt are sown in many young, previously innocent minds.

A friend of mine called me the other day to tell me that she had given her child, a seven-year-old girl, a playful spank on the bum. To her surprise the child said, "Don't you touch me there, Mommy." She had recently attended one of the "good touch/bad touch" programs. This is not an isolated incident. Given the present laws, if that child entered school the following day and told her teacher that her mother had touched her "private parts," the teacher would have been legally compelled to report suspected abuse. Conceivably it could have taken months to determine through the courts that the touch was innocently misconstrued by the child and the teacher. Yet, the compounded errors that result in this kind of scenario are the consequence of programs and systems that have only the best interests of the child at heart.

Nonetheless, one cannot help feeling skeptical at times. With the phenomenal rise in the reported incidence of child sexual abuse, psychotherapists have had a growth industry on their hands. A great many people with dubious qualifications have hung out shingles as counsellors, consultants, and therapists. In Minnesota, one of the hardest-hit states with regard to sexual-abuse charges, Corey L. Gordon, a lawyer who has been involved in many child-abuse cases, indicated that "Each locality has developed its own body of people claiming expertise. They claim they can establish the truth or falsity of such allegations and, if the allegations are true, bring the child back to health. So, where before you had all these people scrambling to make a living, now they've got more work than they can do, and they're collecting eighty or ninety dollars an hour either from taxpayers or insurance plans." The problem is that legal and academic officials themselves are too deeply involved in the panic atmosphere surrounding the issue to separate the good from the bad — and not just in terms of touch.

One cannot argue with the fact that the number of reports of child sex abuse has increased tenfold during the last decade and, even allowing for false allegations, thousands of children are getting needed help that wasn't available a short time ago. However, one has to be concerned that at every level, contacts between children and adults are becoming tainted with suspicion and fear. Men in particular face a new spectrum of hostilities and self-doubts. They have become "the enemy." And in our haste to "solve" this problem we accept "treatment" recommendations that should profoundly disturb a democratic society.

The two major treatment programs in use in North America (which differ only in details) were set out by Henry Giaretto and Suzanne Sgroi, two highly respected child advocates. In their ideal world, innovative child-care practitioners need to be skilled, well-educated people who have come to terms with their own sexuality and feeling toward the sexual exploitation of children. Both programs rely heavily on former victims of abuse who have been through extensive healing processes as counsellors and spokespeople, since they understand the meaning of abuse and empathize with the victims. Sgroi and Giaretto identify a number of tasks that belong to the social work domain, including changing the value system of the community, both among individuals and professionals, concerning the sexual abuse of children (that is, they support the new perspective that has been discussed above); integrating the industry's disparate workers, such as law enforcement officers, Crown prosecutors, specialized therapists, psychologists, etc.; engaging victims in prolonged and intensive treatment programs with their significant oth-ers — siblings, parents, relatives, etc.; establishing preventive programs aimed at children and adults who interact with them, such as teachers, to help them understand sexual abuse and to assure children that responsible adults will listen and take appropriate protective action when children complain of abuse.[17]

This is Sgroi and Giaretto's rather noble plan to effectively change the environment that generates and misunderstands the abused child. It is an ambitious social program. Commu-nity education to achieve a change in values is necessary in light of the tradition of disbelief that has silenced children about the genuine abuses they have suffered. Today, a child should be able to go to a parent, teacher, minister, relative, or counsellor who will "believe her, listen sympathetically, and finally take effective action to end the abuse in a way [that does] not further damage the child's self-esteem."[18] Once a child reports abuse, an appropriate child-welfare agency should be notified, and the police informed. The underlying goal of the investigation should be to serve the best interests of a damaged, unhappy, and traumatized young person, and the goal of all action should be to enable the child to recover his or her sense of dignity, self-respect, and self-esteem. In theory, this seems like an ideal response to the question of how to deal reasonably and effectively with all parties involved in an abusive situation. But in practice, it often doesn't work that way.

This all-encompassing treatment model is being used in most major American cities, and has been adopted by most Canadian Children's Aid Society (CAS) officials, to the extent that resources and education allow. According to the optimis-tic scenarios, a Canadian child would understand when abuse had taken place, report it to sympathetic authorities, be assured of a remedy, and not find it necessary to "endure [a] gruelling cross-examination in court. The best judicial systems are those in which social workers, having interviewed the child, can give evidence by proxy."[19] To this end, Canadian child advocates are educating children through the schools about "good and bad" touch, enlightening teachers and other professionals about the signs of sexual abuse, and entering the courtrooms armed with their knowledge and a commitment to changing the existing order. And this, despite the best intentions, is where we get to the root of the problem.

Like their counterparts in the United States, the majority of Canadian social workers and child advocates accept the premise that children do not lie about sexual abuse. As stated earlier, this dogma was first formulated by Roland Summit in his now-famous book, *The Child Sexual Abuse Accommodation Syndrome*. Children who have been abused, but are reluctant to say anything about it, will display a number of indicative behaviors, such as night tremors, bed-wetting, precocious sexual knowledge, depression, hyperactivity, overly compliant behavior, acting out or aggressive behavior, pseudomature behavior, arriving early at school and leaving it late, lack of trust, inability to concentrate, eating disorders, a drop in school performance, and so on. Unless the child were perfectly adjusted, it would appear that almost any behavior that he or she could engage in might signal sexual abuse to a suspicious observer. Such children, teachers and social workers are cautioned, should be suspected of having been sexually abused. Not all the symptoms need appear, but any of them should arouse suspicion and trigger an appropriate set of questions. Sexual-abuse investigators are also aware that children do not naturally like to talk about abuse for a variety of reasons; thus, one must be gentle, but diligent, in helping them to disclose their secrets. Sgroi even counsels lying to get at the truth, if necessary.[20]

But once such a complex, perhaps devious, investigative process is put into practice, that process itself will tend to evoke the responses that make up the "accommodation syndrome": secrecy; helplessness; entrapment; accommodation;

delayed, conflicting, and unconvincing disclosure; and retraction. Furthermore, the responses that one would expect from a child where abuse had *not* occurred are also the symptoms that are said to constitute the sexual abuse accommodation syndrome: the child will deny it, or "attempt to keep it secret," but, after repeated questionings, will finally begin to "confess", in progressively elaborate detail, to precisely those things the social workers have been asking about.

The heart of this dilemma was stated — albeit somewhat confusedly — by a California judge, the Honorable Robert T. Baca. He was responding to a motion to exclude an accused father from the trial when his daughter was testifying, on the grounds that his presence might intimidate the child into retracting her testimony — which, while considered true by the investigating agency, had still to be assessed by the judge, the final arbiter of justice. After listening to the girl's testimony, the leading questions of her lawyer, and the children-don't-lie theory espoused by the sexual-abuse experts, Judge Baca said:

> Well . . . you can make that interpretation . . . also if they . . . vehemently deny it. . . . If a child denies that sexual activity takes place we are to assume that it is a lie, that it did take place. And then if they say it took place, we are to assume that a child never tells a lie. Is that the situation? If a child says that sexual activity took place, we have to accept it without question, but if they deny it took place we have to assume without question that it is a lie.[21]

It is a very confusing dogma. Once you apply the theory of the sexual abuse accommodation syndrome to children's statements, then nothing they say can count against the belief that the abuse happened. If they deny it initially, that's because they have to keep it secret. If they first admit and then deny it, that's because they are helpless, confused, and frightened. If they first deny, then admit, and later retract it, that is also evidence that they were abused. Everything the child does is evidence of sexual abuse. According to Sgroi, the important idea to get across to the child is that the investigator/interviewer believes that the abuse did happen, and is not going to go away before getting to the bottom of it. As she put it, "my kids get the message that this broad ain't gonna go away until she gets what she wants." What she wants is an admission of sexual abuse that she already believes has happened. But if no abuse actually happened, the enforced discussion of strange and tainted sexuality can seriously retard the child's development and affect his or her relationship with the accused adult. In many cases, the accused succumbs to the urge to plea bargain — to admit guilt and seek "appropriate treatment," just to get the whole process to end. Treatment, at that point, becomes punishment.

VOCAL, the national U.S. association organized in opposition to the onslaught of false accusations, has received hundreds of letters claiming innocence and violation of parental rights. The theme of these letters revolves around the violence done by the state through the mandated child-protection legislation. They recount the destruction of families, bankruptcies, forced plea bargains, children taken away (often permanently), social alienation, termination of jobs, loss of business and homes, threats of violence, social ostracization, vandalism of property, and stress-induced illnesses. One man committed suicide rather than live with the accusation. Once accused, both in Canada and the United States, the individuals' names are placed on an abuse register; even if they are later found innocent, their names remain on the register and can only be removed after a costly legal fight.

To the public, suspected child molesters are equated with rapists and other sexual deviants. The public feels they deserve whatever punishment they get. Such people become the lepers of their communities. Friends become enemies, wives turn against their husbands, and children rise up against their parents.

It is a vicious circle. As more and more cases are reported, more and more people tend to believe that an increasingly large number of children are being abused. The more belief, the greater the mistrust; and the greater the mistrust, the more cause for suspicion and accusation. Factor in the children-don't-lie doctrine, and a full-scale, institutionalized national witch-hunt becomes not only possible, but probable. This is what is now happening.

To ask whether or not children lie about sexual abuse is misleading as well as mistaken. Rather, as was noted by Minnesota psychologist Ralph Underwager, given the plastic and malleable nature of children, the question should be "what degree, kind, and type of influence has been exerted upon them?" This does not necessarily mean that a deliberate and malicious intent on the part of an adult is required to trigger the kind of influence that will result in shaping, moulding, and essentially teaching a child to produce a tale that is false. As Underwager puts it, "The essential engineering or fabrication of a false allegation can result from intent to do good, coupled with a preconceived idea of what has happened and a lack of awareness of the susceptibility of children to [the influence of] adult authority figures." In the atmosphere of mistrust and hysteria surrounding child sexual abuse, the beliefs of the authority figures the child encounters during a lengthy period of interrogation become imprinted on the child's mind. A child who is interviewed in the manner that Suzanne Sgroi advocates would be influenced by what he or she believed to be what the interviewer wanted to hear. And it would be very clear that what the interviewer wanted to hear about was sexual abuse.

It is important at this point to see how the combination of the ideal Sgroi–Giaretto scenario mentioned above, the mounting concern over abuse, and the belief that children don't lie works in practice.

The processes of bringing a suspected abuser to justice, and a child victim to truth and therapy, are much the same in both Canada and the United States. In Canada, a step-by-step approach is set out in the *Child Abuse/Neglect Policy Handbook* that was published by Ontario's Ministry of Human Resources in 1980, and updated four years later to incorporate newly gained knowledge about sexual abuse. Guidelines and protocol pamphlets are available to the public and to professionals through the Ministry of Community and Social Services and the Ontario Centre for the Prevention of Child Abuse. What follows then is the purely clinical modus operandi of the Canadian social worker. There will be minor differences between the provinces, but overall the procedures are the same.

Every person who has reasonable grounds to believe that a child is in need of protection is obligated to inform an appropriate child welfare agency. Professionals face a $1,000 penalty for failing to report suspected child abuse. Thus, complaints may come from teachers, doctors, law enforcement officers, daycare workers, and other professionals. Spouses too are now frequently lodging complaints. And in Vancouver, an abuse hotline allows a complaint to be made anonymously over the phone. Policy and practice concerning hotline calls is to err on the side of caution.

The social worker is encouraged to react immediately to a complaint, usually beginning with a search through the Child Abuse Registry, where previous complaints — substantiated or not — have been recorded. Discussion may be necessary with other resource persons, such as school or probation officers. The police must be notified; the accused offender is then confronted, usually by both the worker and the police. The child is interviewed separately from the parental figures to prevent their exerting pressure on the child to recant the story. Depending on the outcome of this confrontation, the social worker will assess the risk to the child, based upon factors such as the child's age, evidence of injury, and relationship to parents, along with the parents' methods of discipline, verbal statements, admission of guilt, etc. The social worker must then make the difficult decision as to whether the offending adult's guarded or hostile reaction represents righteous indignation at an unfair complaint, or an attempt to cover up guilt.

While the safety and well-being of the child are the paramount considerations, the social worker must consider some of the following questions in determining whether to remove the child from the situation or to provide remedial preventative services without resorting to the court process: How serious is the alleged abuse or neglect? Is it an isolated incident, or are there likely to be future occurrences? Are the parents capable of, and amenable to, altering their pattern of dealing with their children with the assistance of child-care workers, parent-training groups, financial help, or any other remedial service that the worker can offer?

The only criterion necessary for deciding to remove the child from the home is that the worker "reasonably believe[s] that the child is in need of protection." The social worker may see removal as a necessary course of action in a number of cases. Section 1 of the *Child Abuse/Neglect* manual describes some of the indicators that a child is in need of protection: abuse or neglect such that the child's safety or well-being is endangered; abandonment; deprivation of necessary care through death, absence, or disability of the parents; deprivation of medical attention; and so on. The most commonly used reason is "inability to parent" — a catch-all phrase that can be fleshed out by details discovered through investigation. In this vague term lies the formidable power of the social worker, and its very imprecision provides ample opportunity for misuse of that power.

When a social worker believes that a child has been abused, sexually or otherwise, and is in danger of further abuse if allowed to remain in the home, that worker will remove the child to a temporary foster or other institutional home, and continue with the investigation. Within ten days the social worker must file a report to the courts, where the options for further action will be considered and, if necessary, a trial ordered. Between the time the child is removed from the home and the day — usually months, sometimes years, later — that the case is finally judged in family court on the "balance of probabilities," the accused are treated as if guilty until proven otherwise.

"Apprehending the child" — the official term for removing the child from the home — initiates a legal process. Medical examinations, psychiatric reports, remarks by school officials (and possibly clergy or other members of the community who know the family) will be required to support the state's decisions regarding removal and/or treatment. If a decision to apprehend the child is made, and the parent refuses to co-operate with this action, social workers can apply to a family court judge for a warrant to search the premises, or "enter and apprehend." If the child is perceived to be in immediate danger, a police officer — one of whom will in most provinces accompany the social worker to the home of the accused — is permitted to enter without a warrant and remove the child to a safe environment. The child stays in the custody of a state social agency pending the trial.

In such cases, children are the primary witnesses — often the only witnesses. During the often-lengthy period before the actual court case the child will be questioned by police, foster parents, lawyers, social workers, therapists, physicians, psychiatrists, and others, many of whom are predisposed to believe that the child has been abused.

The first official interview of a child may involve anything from a single social worker questioning the child in a "neutral environment" (that is, someplace other than the home) to a group of social workers, police officers, and prosecutors — and in the United States, at least, the media. The alleged abuser usually is not allowed to see the child. The interrogation may be conducted in an official place, or in the office of a person deemed to be an expert in dealing with child sexual abuse. Separated from familiar surroundings, children tend to lose their bearings and become more and more dependent on the new authority figures. As the isolation and interrogation continue children learn what the adults around them want to know. They learn the language of sexual abuse; and they learn how to play the role of victim.

Interrogations of any sort are heavily weighted in favor of the powerful authority figure, who assumes that certain things have happened, and organizes the interrogation around those assumptions. The bias of even the most skilled investigator will necessarily affect not only the course of the questions, but the responses provided by the child.

In this context, investigators are encouraged to ignore a child's statements that nothing happened. Responses that tend to confirm the hypothesis that the child was abused are rewarded with smiles, playful rapport, promises, etc. The highly suggestible child is given rather obvious clues as to what the interviewer/interrogator wants to hear.

In cases involving three- to seven-year-old children, many interviewers also use "anatomically correct" dolls to guide the child's description of the alleged sexual abuse. Psychologist Ralph Underwager, writing about interrogation procedures in American child sex abuse trials, states that "there has been no research whatsoever to verify or establish the reliability and validity of [such] dolls as assessment or evaluation tools. A search of all relevant professional literature indexes, computer databases, and retrieval systems did not locate a single research study on the use of these dolls." Suzanne Sgroi agrees that there is no valid research on the use of anatomically correct dolls; however, she encourages their use with younger children to assist them in telling their story.

In reality, these dolls are not anatomically correct. Their genitals are enormously exaggerated and, combined with the interviewer's constant questioning about sexual abuse, they alert the child, consciously or unconsciously, that the interviewer is interested solely in sexuality — and moreover, in "bad" sexuality. The interviewing methods that Sgroi recommends are explicitly suggestive. The dolls are handed to the child, who is expected to undress them spontaneously. If the child does not do so, then he or she should be encouraged to. If the child still does not undress the dolls, then the interviewer should undress them, and help the child explore them. Four naked dolls, two male and two female, are used; all of them have enlarged "anatomically correct" genital areas. The child is then prompted to tell the interviewer what happened. Transcripts of many child sexual abuse investigations demonstrate that identification of sexual parts and naming of the abuser are rewarded with comments like "That's right" or "Very good," or with favorable comments that call for more explicit information. Such responses once again elicit from the suggestible, confused child those statements that they have learned are acceptable. Repeated interviews concerning different aspects of sexual abuse give children the clear negative message that all the authority figures around them want to hear about sexual abuse.

The difficult concept to grasp here is that it does not necessarily require a deliberate or malicious intent on the part of the adult to trigger the kind of influence that results in such shaping of the child's tale, which essentially teaches the child to produce an account that is false. But we need only recall psychologist Ralph Underwager's suggestion that, despite their "intent to do good," the investigators' "preconceived idea of what happened" combined with our "lack of awareness of the susceptibility of children" to adult influence can often result in false allegations being made.

To understand the effects of all this on the flesh-and-blood realities of daily life, we can consider the 1986 case of a Vancouver-based Mormon couple, Wanita and Maurice Gareau. The seven Gareau children were removed from their home after a third-hand allegation of abuse was reported to a child-welfare worker. At issue was a foster mother's reporting to a social worker that her foster daughter, a friend of one of the Gareau daughters, had told her about an alleged sexual incident between Maurice Gareau and one of his daughters. Three social workers went to the daughter's school, interviewed other friends of the children, and decided "in good faith" that the seven Gareau children should be removed from their home. There were no independent witnesses. The Gareaus were not allowed to speak with their children before the social workers removed them, nor were they allowed to house the children among friends in their religious community. The social workers threatened Wanita Gareau with jail if she did not give up the children. The parents' names were placed on the Child Abuse Registry list, and they were forced to go to court, where it was eventually decided that no abuse had taken place. The girls admitted to having been "confused" by the social workers. At no time during this entire process did they indicate that their father had abused them.

In 1986 the Gareaus sued the three social workers, claiming that the "seizure provisions of the *Family and Child Service Act* violate the Charter of Rights and Freedoms." They also sought damages for "false imprisonment, distress and suffering, and for defamation of character" because their names remained on the Child Abuse Registry list. The British Columbia attorney general's office argued that the social workers were acting "in good faith" and that therefore there was no misconduct on their part. What this, and the many cases like it, tells us, is that social workers, despite the best of intentions, have an enormous authority which they can abuse.

Or, take the case of the Elliot Lake couple who fell into the zealous hands of the Catholic Children's Aid Society. Their child was considered in need of protection from his abusive parents by a group of experts from the Hospital for Sick Children who misdiagnosed a rare bone disease as the result of severe child abuse. They did not accept the parents' explanation. In this case, the judge ordered that the child be placed in the care of his grandmother. When it was finally proved that the child was suffering from a rare bone disorder, the child was returned, and the parents vindicated to some degree. They were awarded $4,400 in legal costs. Judge Peter Nasmith said, at the time, that the Society's conduct was indefensible. He also had harsh words for the child-abuse team that had misdiagnosed the child's condition. His final comments bear repeating in full, as they point to the crux of what we have been examining here:

> The zeal of the well-meaning people, who are so understandably devoted to fighting the scourge that is child-abuse, must be scrutinized by a protection agency and courts. This zeal has created a subtle dynamic that can somehow convert a suspicion of child-abuse into a presumption of child-abuse. . . . This must be quite frightening to the citizens of a free and democratic society.

4
SATANISM:
Salem Revisited

Witch-hunt *n* **1: A searching out and persecution of persons accused of witchcraft 2: An investigation of or campaign against dissenters (as political opponents) conducted on the pretext of protecting the public welfare and resulting in public persecution and defamation of character.**
Webster's Third New International Dictionary

Señores, it does not help to say that I did it, and I have admitted that what I have done has brought me to this suffering — Señor, you know the truth — Señor, for God's sake, have mercy on me. Señor, take these things from my arms. . . . They are killing me.
Inquisition interviewee, 1670 (from *The Damned Art*, Sydney Anglo)

Allegations of grossly deviant sexuality coupled with the ritual murder and mutilation of children are not new to Western civilization. They are as ancient as our oldest myths, and evoke the same stark terror today as in the past among those who hear rumors of the practice. But where does our current knowledge of these practices come from?

It comes from children. It comes from members of society whom we have labelled insane — such as schizophrenics or persons who suffer from the strange disease known as multiple-personality disorder. Occasionally demonic imagery is given form by our artists. And less frequently it is spoken of by members of cults that actually practice diabolical rites. When such self-confessed cultists speak, evidence is

107

usually found. Children and the mentally aberrant, however, appear to be speaking from some deep level of the psyche. Freud posited that these dark fantasies are primordial images lifted out of the seething mass of instinctual urges that are active below the threshold of consciousness. Jung would tell us that they are archetypes — ancient, dynamic symbols of the unconscious mind, that we can tap into with both good and bad results, depending on how prepared we are. Both men went among the insane or neurotic in order to learn more about this phenomenon of the mind.

Still, when children speak of these things, one asks if it is conceivable that children could imaginatively group together a cluster of depraved activities that have always been associated with pagans, witches, and satanic cults? This question, if divorced from the more obvious religious or psychological context in which these fantasies almost always appear, is not easy to answer. Therefore, in order to get a sense of the larger picture, it is necessary to achieve some perspective by entering into our own dark history. We must look at the sources of the volatile mixture of fact and nightmarish fantasy.

Father Frank LeBar, a New York priest who acts as a consultant on cults for the Vatican, contends that over the last few years there has been a "dramatic rise in the number of young people who are drawn into this nebulous world." He calls the phenomenon "a rapidly growing problem."[1] He points to the visibility of satanic symbols on toys and television and the philosophy of satanic ritual and practice invoked by and disseminated through "heavy-metal" music. He points with alarm to the rising number of suicide attempts by teenagers, many of whom have made explicit statements associating their actions with their satanic beliefs. In Father LeBar's diocese, a number of parents have been scandalized to hear their children mouthing slogans like "Satan is in and God is out." He too is aware of the increase in allegations of ritual killings and organized molestation groups and in the number of criminals whose acts appear to have satanic overtones. His

alarm grew in the spring of 1986 when he was asked to participate in a conference for the helping professions that was to
examine the ritualistic sexual abuse of children. "From that
conference I concluded that the problem is more widespread
than anybody could imagine. The children who are involved
are often so young that people wonder if they are making it all
up. There are very rarely bodies, and young children are
considered by the courts to be unreliable witnesses, so it is
very difficult to prosecute these cases. I believe it is a significant problem and if the signs are correct it is going to get
worse." In others words, Father LeBar, like many of the others
who believe these accounts, has seen no evidence.

Charles Macleod, research co-ordinator for Montreal's
Cult Project, an education and resource center on cultism,
agrees that satanism is becoming a fad among young people
in the 1980s. But he believes that the allegations of ritual
abuse, though alarming, are in need of more concrete evidence. Like every other agency that is investigating allegations of ritual abuse and murder, Macleod expresses concern
about this distinct lack of physical evidence substantiating
the claims that are being made. "Sure the interest is there," he
says, "but the lack of hard-and-fast evidence should stop us
from jumping to conclusions."

But for many observers, this lack of evidence does not
hamper belief. Bette Naysmith, research and law enforcement representative of the U.S. Cult Awareness Network, con-
siders the lack of evidence a result of the diabolical practice
of cannibalism itself: "Satanists," she says, "are eating the
evidence!" She holds this rather astonishing conviction for
the same reason the judge and psychiatrists in the Hamilton
case believed the children: it is hard to imagine how children
as young as five years of age could offer detailed accounts of
the ceremonial mutilation of bodies and the ritual practices
of satanic cults, unless they had themselves participated in
these activities.

It is not difficult to believe that there are satanic cults, or psychotic personalities who align themselves with satanism. Investigators occasionally find the stinking remains of bodies buried in some sadist's cave-like basement, or a woman chained to a wall who tells of the tortures she suffered at the hands of a sadistic man or cult. But in the majority of the cases where children utter their horrifying thoughts, no evidence is found.

Dr. John Mead, a California child psychologist who has studied nearly one hundred such tales told by children, posits that some traumatic event (not necessarily sexual abuse) has caused these children to regress to primitive fantasies of evil. He cites case after case in which children tell incredibly detailed stories of molestation, cannibalism, and murder, only to recant them much later. Schizophrenics, he observes, show the same tendency to regress to lower levels of the mind — what Freud called the "id"; in this state they manifest rage, hatred, and fear of devils and cannibalism. The trigger for such fantasies in children might be something as simple as "a child being taken away from his parents or being asked during a stressful period if a parent molested him." Any kind of sustained stress, Mead contends, can subvert the normal functioning of the mind, causing it to regress to a more primitive state.[2]

Dr. Otto Weininger, a professor at the Ontario Institute for Studies in Education (OISE) who has worked with abused children since the early 1970s, believes that, for the most part, many of the therapists now dealing with these children simply aren't properly trained in children's development. "Children come up with horrific fantasies on a routine basis", Weininger explains. "That is simply a part of their inner development. These things like cannibalism, cooking babies — quite diverse, destructive images — are part of their psychological makeup. ... Parents and therapists often tell me of the rather grotesque things that children have told them and I have to tell them that it's just not that abnormal. I think in the kinds of cases you're seeing now, people are hearing these

things who aren't equipped to deal with this aspect of children's thinking, and they tend to overreact."[3]

Doris Bell, the California woman who encouraged her two
grandchildren to tell tales of ritual abuse, provides a good
example of how the prior belief of an interviewer can eventually wrest a supposed "secret" from a child. The initial interviewer's own fears and questions inspire the fantasy life of
suggestible children and lead them to tell tales. The fantasy
becomes "fact" as soon as it is believed. The consequences of
this process are disturbing. If believed, the child is encouraged to say more, confirming the suspicions of the interviewer. And the convinced investigator must look for the
culprits. But because they don't really exist, he or she must
invent them. Depending on the time, place, and historical
context, the culprits may be witches, satanists, or cultists; or, as
in the present context, satanic child sexual abusers. Those in
the helping professions persuade people like Father LeBar
that these kinds of practices cannot be dismissed, that they
are happening far more often than we would like to believe.
In turn Father LeBar becomes one more zealous member of
the community warning parents and priests to watch for sex
abuse and satanic practices among children. Parents in turn
begin to watch for behavior that fits neatly into the theory.
When they find it, they tell LeBar, who investigates along with
other helping professionals, all of whom are predisposed to
believe that satanic sexual abuse happened. It is a widening
circle of self-replicating belief, none of which is based on
tangible evidence. This is the how this legend, based on exaggerated fact and embroidered by paranoid fantasy, has spread
across North America. This is the humble beginning of an
hysterical purpose. This is the prelude to an institutionalized
witch-hunt.

All of the theories proposed to explain this phenomenon
are debatable. One can choose to believe that cannibals eat
the evidence, that children are regressing to phylogenetic
realms of the mind, or that they are merely reflecting back to

the authority figures around them something that says more about the authorities' state of mind than anything else. But the final arbiter of truth must be material evidence.

The effect of material evidence may be best exemplified by the Frank Fuster case in Dade County, Florida. More than a dozen children testified that Fuster had sexually assaulted them. The judge had to ask, were the children's statements the product of fact or fantasy? A man's life depended upon the answer to that question. He finally decided that they were fact, based on the material evidence: Fuster's son had been found to have gonorrhea of the throat. But in other cases, innocent people are accused and convicted without a scrap of material evidence. And they have no recourse in such matters.

By taking a long step back into our past we may obtain a sobering perspective from which to view the present moral panic about sex abuse generally and satanic abuse specifically. Because it may help us to avoid the hysteria generated by three young girls that transformed a small religious town like Salem, Massachusetts, into a witch-hunter's paradise, this is a necessary digression. While our concern for children is justified, the current climate of fear is leading us to act unwisely. Society is trampling on civil rights that have evolved over the centuries, rights that separate us from the rule of tyrants.

Human sacrifice, cannibalism, and unrestrained sexuality are common motifs in many religious rituals all over the world. But it was the Greek pagan tradition, as filtered through Roman Catholicism, that was carried across Europe and became the reference point when the medieval mind thought about these non-Christian practices. According to Greek mythology, Kronos — father of Zeus and one of the most powerful among the Greek pantheon of gods — attempted to devour all of his divine children. Human sacrifices were offered to the Greek god Dionysus, and sexual orgies were practiced by most of his female followers. Those who refused to worship Dionysus were supposedly driven mad by his devotees, who would tear them to pieces before devouring them. Dionysus himself, the horned god, half-man, half-animal, had supposedly been thrown into a cauldron of boiling water, dismembered, and partially eaten by his faithful followers, who then scattered his remains over the ground in a sacrificial ceremony reminiscent of fertility cults throughout the world. According to the myths, followers of Dionysus re-enacted this sacrifice at their gatherings, where after the frenzied devouring of human flesh, they would abandon themselves to a day-long sexual orgy.

But although the sacrifice of children and the eating of their flesh were common in myth and legend, in actuality such practices were regarded as heinous crimes, utterly taboo in civilized societies. In his *Nicomachean Ethics*, Aristotle lists among other unnatural criminals "those who provide children for one another to eat." Early Christians railed against "those who eat their own and other children," while persecuting Romans accused them of precisely the same crimes.

Dionysus represented carnal urges, a celebration of unrestrained sensuality and sexuality: a man–animal combination that paralleled this image became the most popular depiction of Satan in Christian teaching. Other pagan ceremonies that were close in spirit to the Dionysian, whether Druidic or Nordic in origin, similarly represented to early Christian clerics everything in the sinful world from which they were trying to escape.

This picture of Satan continued to evolve during the Dark Ages. Sex, indulgence in delicate or excessive food and drink, communal gatherings and dances, frivolity, remnants of pagan festivals, and general carnal enjoyments — each of these practices was progressively challenged by the Church, as an increasingly restrictive view of the "straight-and-narrow" path to salvation emerged. The devil was painted as a resourceful, cunning, and dangerously evil being whose temptations to sin would enter human minds through an excess of those activities that were, in moderation, most normal. By the fourteenth century, the beginning of the witch-hunts, the devil was believed capable of transforming himself into a beautiful young man (or woman) and in this guise seducing unwitting human beings, usually women. This equating of the devil with unbridled sexuality became the core theme of demonological literature. And with this back-ground of pagan sacrificial rituals and myths, mixed with primitive Christian beliefs, the equating of pleasurable, devi-ant sexuality with murder and cannibalism became wide-spread at all levels of society.

The concept of the witch or paramour of the devil also continued to exist along with Christian doctrines. This belief too, was based on pre-Christian fables and Greek myths of humans who consorted with gods, and on the Christian teach-ing of Eve's succumbing to the wily Satan's blandishments. But until the early medieval period — the period that will concern us here — the conflict between Christian and pagan beliefs remained latent for long periods of time, despite occa-sional half-hearted attempts by the Church to eradicate pagan beliefs. Only when the Church's temporal power had been sufficiently consolidated did it attempt to attack system-atically any deviation from orthodox belief and practice.

Organized under papal authority in the second half of the thirteenth century and staffed in large part by members of the Dominican order, the Inquisition became the Catholic Church's legal device to deal with the crime of heresy. Among their various activities, the investigators searched out unor-thodox thinkers and destroyed their libraries, and persecuted minority sects and ethnic groups such as Jews. Their system-atic search for witches will concern us here.

It is still difficult for us to comprehend the mentality that permitted supposed "witches" to be hunted down and tor-tured. An understanding of the religious context helps: to the medieval mind, the world was a permanent battleground between the forces of good and evil, with God and Satan as the two supernatural powers engaged in a titanic struggle for control of the world. In keeping with the account of the fall in Genesis, women were seen as the "weak link" in this war — a sort of fifth column through which Satan could infiltrate God's earthly domain.

But religion provides only the beginning of an explanation. Sociology advances it further. In an extremely poor, primarily rural society, women became dispensable creatures once they were past child-bearing age. This was especially true if they were widows or physically incapacitated in any way — they were simply a drain on a perennially feeble economy. In many cultures, women were seen as mere chattels of their husbands; and girls were "less valuable" than boys. It is not surprising then that almost invariably, accused witches were either older, unattached women, or teenage girls. Killing women was thus a mechanism for eliminating burdens on the economy, and at the same time served as a release valve, in a rigidly patriarchal society, for a suppressed fear and hatred of the sexuality and fertility represented by women.

The final element in a possible explanation — and one that helps tie the analysis to the present phenomenon — is the concept of social malaise. From the fourteenth to the seventeenth centuries, the height of the witch-hunting craze, Europe was ravaged by death and pestilence. Deep anxieties about death permeated this peculiar period of history. Such anxiety was set off by the plague pandemic, along with the hordes of crusading warriors that raped and pillaged towns at whim. From the mid-thirteenth century onwards, the Black Death paid repeated visits to most parts of the continent, with devastating results. At least 20 per cent of Europe's estimated population of seventy million disappeared in the first onslaught, and the plague returned roughly once each generation for the better part of three centuries. The extent to which this daily background of death and misery affected the popular mind can be seen in the extreme forms of behavior — such as roving bands of flagellants, and the tens of thousands of persons who were afflicted with St. Vitus's Dance, which caused them, literally, to dance madly to their death — that have been chronicled in the documents and art of the time.[4]

The socio-psychological context in which the witch-hunts appeared was one permeated with fear of uncontrollable death, decay, and violence. Here we can see a parallel to our contemporary situation, in which an entire civilization lives precariously in the shadow of the nuclear bomb and of plagues like AIDS that defy our present knowledge. It is not coincidence that the same kinds of allegations emerged then among the confessed witches as are emerging now among children, or that children, then as now, were often instigators of the witch-hunts. Then as now, social institutions sanctioned this irrational search for and belief in the satanic.

By the fifteenth century, the notion of the witch as the devil's evil consort had entered the parlance of "Everyman" as a matter of fact, if not of faith. By signing a demonic pact, thereby renouncing God and Christianity, she became, it was believed, the devil's servant, a partner in his universal war against all that was good in God's world. She was thought to show her subservience to Satan by becoming his willing sexual slave. Flying through the air at night, she would join others of her kind at mass meetings known as witches' sabbats, where they were said to worship by blaspheming God, copulating with their master, and indulging in sexual orgies. These heretics supposedly practiced secret rites, trampled on the crucifix, spat out communion bread, and slaughtered innocent children. Such people, according to the Church, deserved no mercy: God sanctioned their deaths.

According to an early and well-respected church father, St. Jerome, a woman was "the gateway to the devil, the path of wickedness, the sting of the serpent — in a word, an evil thing." It was a typical and much repeated view. The authors of *Malleus Maleficarum* (The Hammer of Witches), the most comprehensive witch-hunters' manual, wrote that "women are inferior physically, mentally, and morally; thus they have extraordinary difficulty warding off sinful temptations. They have an insatiable carnal lust and are inclined to deception, resist discipline, and lure men into sin and destruction."[5] A judge speaking to his peers in 1590 found it "not unreasonable that this scum of humanity [i.e., witches] should be drawn chiefly from the feminine sex." Historians estimate that four out of five convicted witches were women.

This was the stereotype of the witch that evolved; this was the cluster of characteristics that inquisitors would look for when attempting to extract a confession from an accused person. In Spain, France, Germany, Italy, Sweden, England, and Scotland, in varying degrees and at different times, entire communities hunted down this paramour of the devil and cast her from their midst, even as Christ had once cast out demons and instructed his disciples to do the same in his name. The slaughter continued for centuries, edging its way into very different cultures whose only connection was their Christian belief (which by late medieval times had lost all semblance to the gospel of Jesus Christ). This was the period of Galileo and Shakespeare, of Descartes and Bacon, of Michelangelo and Leonardo da Vinci. It was the dawning of a new era, economically, socially, and culturally. It was, as has often been said, the flowering of Western civilization that opened up into the world we live in today. And yet most of the learned men of the day were solidly in favor of the witch-hunt. Out of this background the inquisitors emerged.

Educated, politically astute, and religious, these men were not in their own minds fighting against old women, but against a social phenomenon that they could not understand. Investigators of the period occasionally questioned whether the flying out at night was fact or fantasy, but they decided, as we do now, that such evil thoughts were not native to the mind and therefore, fact or fantasy, they were products of the devil. But once the wave of accusations and mass hysteria had been set in motion, they themselves were almost unwittingly carried along by it. Their only refuge was to stick with the familiar concepts. And thus arose the standard procedure, which we will now examine, of asking the same questions over and over, of trying to obtain a confession to a litany of sins that was always known beforehand.

Although the details of medieval beliefs in Satan and witches make fascinating reading, we have not gone into them here for their own sake. Rather, this digression was intended to set the background for a comparison of the methods used by the inquisitors and modern abuse investigators, in order to highlight a dangerous trend and a weakness of present-day investigations. That will occupy the rest of this chapter.

The inquisitor's methods of extracting information from suspected witches are well documented. A suspected heretic was informed through the parish priest that she was to report to the Inquisition's nearest office. The priest would then repeat the charges at Mass the following Sunday and for three successive Sundays or feast days. The suspect was then required to present herself to the inquisitor's office and was imprisoned while awaiting trial. Refusal to appear meant excommunication, and to be excommunicated was to be ostracized within the community or hunted down. Anyone who reported the heretic's whereabouts would be rewarded with up to three years of indulgences for their information; those who knew but did not reveal information leading to the arrest of a suspected heretic would be tried for heresy themselves.

Interrogations were carried out in the presence of two religious officials. The public were never admitted. We still have records of many of the interrogations. One of the most disturbing elements of this process was the total secrecy that enshrouded it: the accused rarely knew the names of her accusers or of the prosecution witnesses. Defence was a matter of chance, with the sharp and sophisticated inquisitors designing a battery of leading questions meant to entrap and coerce the accused into a confession of satanic activity. Questions revolved around the pact with the devil, the night rides to the sabbat, the sexual orgy, and the eating of Christian children. Frequently, deviant sexual practices such as sodomizing local children were part of the compendium of charges.

It wasn't enough simply to confess her own pact with the devil: the accused was required to reveal information about her colleagues in heretical practices. Thus, the trial snowballed as the accused's acquaintances were brought in and, in turn, incriminated new suspects. The heretic's refusal to betray her friends was taken as proof that her conversion had not been complete, which necessitated further interrogation and even torture. The threat of torture was often enough to stimulate a confession. It was the most feared and effective of the inquisitor's formidable arsenal of legal weapons, both psychological and physical.

In 1568 in Spain, a woman was arrested because she refused to eat pork or change her linen on Saturdays: she was accused of being a "Jewish witch." What follows is the record of her torture, condensed from an account written by a notary public who was present.

She said initially that she had done nothing. By the end she was making the classic confession, which included accounts of flying out to the sabbats, whoring with the devil and his horde of demonic followers, practicing malefic (i.e., bad) witchcraft against her accusers, and so on. But the inquisitors wanted more. She was placed on the rack. She pleaded, "Señores, why will you not tell me what I have to say? Señor, put me on the ground — have I not said that I did it all?"

Instructed to tell more, she responded, "I don't remember. Take me away. I did what the witnesses say." She was ordered to tell in detail what the witnesses said.

"Señor, as I have told you, I do not know for certain. I have said that I did all that the witnesses say. Señores, please release me, for I do not remember everything that the witnesses say." Tell it all, she was told.

"Señores, it does not help to say that I did it, and I have

admitted that what I have done has brought me to this suffering — Señor, you know the truth — Señor, for God's sake, have
mercy on me. Señor, take these things from my arms. Señor,
please release me, they are killing me."

She was admonished to téll the truth and the garottes were
tightened. She begged, "Señores, do you not see how these
people are killing me? I did it. For God's sake, let me go." The
ropes were tightened again.[6]

Another typical example comes from a 1687 trial in a small
German village. A midwife, Walpurga Hausmannin, was accused by her neighbors of practicing malefic witchcraft,
which caused them every imaginable type of misfortune associated with pregnancy and childbirth. She had been practicing midwifery for nineteen years in the same community, had
been a widow for three decades, and was looked upon as a bit
of an eccentric. She was unable to answer her accusers'
charges, most of which she had no way of knowing. Thus she
was forced to undergo the full inquisitional treatment. Following the standard procedures, her interrogators asked
whether she knew the Lord's Prayer, the *Ave Maria*, the Apos-
tles' Creed, and the Ten Commandments. She recited all of
them. The next questions were less innocuous: Who had
seduced her into witchcraft? How had this seduction occurred? Why had she given in to the temptation? Where had
all this taken place? What was the devil like? Did it hurt to
have sexual intercourse with him? Why did she not break off
her relationship with him? Whom else had she seduced during her years of service? and so on.

Initially she denied any knowledge of devil worship, sabbats, or other witches. Under torture, however, she confessed
that she had accepted the devil as her master, flown on a
pitchfork during the night to meet with other worshippers,
renounced Christ and God and defamed the sacraments,
blasphemed against the Virgin Mary, and consumed the flesh
of innocent Christian children. By the time they finished with

her, she had named scores of witches whom she said accompanied her on her night rides.[7]

Her confession demonstrates remarkably well the results of the inquisitors' methods of using leading questions to draw out specific information from so-called witches, information that was then used to confirm the existence of witch cults and to convince the world of the reality of sexual servants of the devil. The records clearly showed that after being tortured the witches confessed. To the medieval mind, this signified that torture was justified and that witches existed . . . everywhere. Confession was taken as confirmation, and fantasy became fact.

A few lonely voices of sanity cried for understanding during this hysterical period. One such man, Friedrich von Spree, sent a report to the authorities attacking the witch trial procedures. He wrote, "Among us Germans . . . there are popular superstitions, envy, calumnies, backbiting, insinuations, and the like, which, being neither punished nor refuted over the course of time, stir up accusations of witchcraft. I fear that in many cases we may be mistaken."[8]

In a document written in 1612, at the time of a major witch-hunting outbreak in Navarre, Alonzo Salazar de Frias, a Spanish judge, alleges that he personally checked the claims of 1,802 people who had confessed to witchcraft. He had chemists analyze the so-called magical ointments; he had doctors confirm the virginity of women who claimed to have had intercourse with the devil or his demons. It was discovered that one of the major sabbats had allegedly been taking place on the site on which the secretaries of the Inquisition had been working for years. De Frias concluded that not one act of witchcraft had really occurred, that they were all in the minds of the accused individuals and, most important, "that there were neither witches nor bewitched until they were talked or written about."[9] This unusually clear-headed report managed to allay the drastic effects of the Inquisition in

Navarre at precisely the moment that it was reaching its peak in other parts of Europe. De Frias's salient observation that "neither witches nor bewitched" existed "until they were talked or written about" should be kept in mind when considering present-day, media-induced hysteria concerning satanic child sexual abuse. Today's cult practices began to be discussed in earnest only in the early 1980s. Since then we have had a hundred-fold increase in these kinds of allegations.

Dr. Charles Vincent, who was himself tortured in the course of his duties in China in the 1940s, has written about the psychology of interrogation procedures that employ psychological and/or physical means of torture. He suggests that the interrogation setting is all-important. Removed from familiar surroundings, forced to rely solely upon the interrogator to gain reprieve from the situation, an individual's will is slowly destroyed until, as Vincent puts it so eloquently,

> You are annihilated . . . exhausted. . . . You can't control yourself, or remember what you said two minutes before. You feel that all is lost. . . . From that moment, the judge is the real master of you. You accept anything he says. When he asks how many "intelligences" you gave to that person, you just put out a number in order to satisfy him. If he says, "Just those?" you say, "No, there are more." If he says, "One hundred," you say, "Yes, one hundred." . . . You do whatever they want.[10]

The Salem trials, one of the last outbreaks of witch mania, present an interesting but far from unusual variation on the theme of witch-hunting. The concept of demonic possession was firmly rooted in the gospel accounts of Jesus' driving out of unclean spirits. Theological discussions and stories of people whose bodies had been taken over by demons were set down in manuscript form and became staples of demonological literature. But it was only during the sixteenth and seventeenth centuries, under the influence of proselytizing Protestant reformers, that possession by the devil became a common phenomenon.

Women, usually adolescents, were more prone than men to this condition. In a possessed state they would blaspheme, shirk their imposed religious obligations, and discuss sexual intercourse openly and explicitly. During the possession they showed a complete disregard for all that they had been taught by their pious parents and religious authorities. Often the possessed woman would claim that a witch ordered devils to attack her and inhabit her body. Convents in Europe became famous for the outbreaks of multiple possession that many of the nuns suffered. Children, too, often played a crucial role in establishing the alleged reality of demonic possession.

For example, in Spain, during the Basque witch trials in 1610, hundreds of children confessed to having participated in witches' sabbats. They were so detailed in their accounts of these night-time pursuits that a zealous inquisitor, Pierre Le Dranque, wrote a 200-page account based on their experiences. The account follows in every detail the written lore about the witches' sabbat. His Satanic Majesty is there, with his large penis and scaly skin; the women — 500 of whom were accused by the children and accordingly tried — are said to have engaged in sexual intercourse after devouring the flesh of innocent children, and so on. And, again not surprisingly, the children's experiences followed a period of intense searching for witches, during which priests delivered fiery, colorful sermons, denouncing witches as the scourge of society and describing their habitual practices in detail.[11] A similar occurrence happened in Sweden in 1669 when a royal commission investigated charges of possession in a fifteen-year-old girl. The commission called for sermons and prayers to be said by the Lutheran faithful throughout the girl's province. Thousands of people heard these sermons. And suddenly many children appeared with claims that they too were possessed. They too writhed on the floor, contorted their

bodies into unimaginable positions, and made lewd comments about their elders. The outbreak lasted for several
years, spreading across the country and into neighboring
Swedish-speaking provinces of Finland.

At least eighty-three witchcraft trials took place between
Massachusetts and Virginia from 1647 to 1691; many resulted
in executions. In 1689, Cotton Mather, one of the most zealous and important authorities involved in the Salem trials,
wrote a book about possession based on the trial and execu-
tion of an elderly Irish woman who was accused by three
children in her neighborhood of sending spirits into them.

Three years after Mather's book was published, Abigail
Williams, the eleven-year-old niece of Mather's colleague, the
Reverend Samuel Parris, was playfully experimenting with
crystal balls, a practice much railed against by her puritan
father and other religious reformers in and around her
household. Shortly after engaging in what her father considered "sinful and diabolical magic," Abigail and her friend
Elizabeth began experiencing "odd postures," "fits," and "dis-
tempers."[12] The Reverend Parris sought medical advice. The
physician and other ministers suggested that the disturbance
was "of the devil" and counselled Parris to pray and fast (the
Protestant prescription for demonic possession). As word of
the girls' illness and its probable demonic origin spread
through Parris's circle of friends, other children began to
exhibit similar symptoms. Within two months, seven young
adolescents were said to be possessed, along with one family's
maid and four married women, one of whom was mother and
aunt to two of the young girls.

After weeks of intense questioning by adults, Elizabeth and
Abigail began to claim that they were being tormented by
Tituba, a West Indian servant in the Parris household; by
Sarah Good, a destitute beggar; and by Sarah Osborne, an
unpopular and unorthodox villager.[13] The three women were
arrested and questioned by the elders. Tituba immediately
confessed to extensive dealings with the devil. The others

denied everything. They were held in the Boston jail, where Sarah Osborne died of natural causes within six weeks. Like others who voluntarily confessed, Tituba was released, but Sarah Good refused to admit any wrongdoing. She was the first to be hanged from the gallows. Within five months, five more women would be put to death for refusing to acknowledge that they were witches and the jails were full of many more awaiting trial.

The trials were an ongoing source of horror and fascination. The hearings took place in a frenzy of convulsive seizures and rantings and ravings by the young girls, who were said to be speaking the devil's tongue. Abigail said that there was a "great black man" present with her at the trials, whispering to her what she must say next. On certain days other young girls came to the proceedings, and they too were said to be "greviously afflicted" by the demons. None among the learned elders of the community could understand the girls' strange, convulsive behavior except as the result of witchcraft. All evidence against the accused witches came from the possessed girls, who claimed to be able to tell through "spectral evidence" who was guilty among the accused. On their word alone, twenty persons were executed, and hundreds more were charged. By the time the Governor, whose wife had been accused of witchcraft, put an end to the trials, the entire colony was "afraid that those that sat next to them were under the influence of Witchcraft." (This universal mistrust was precisely what was implied by a Scott County investigator at the conclusion of the Jordan, Minnesota, trials.)

The events in Salem represent a remarkably clear case of prepubescent girls living in a highly restrictive domestic environment that was rife with interpersonal conflict, which generated depressive states and delusional thinking. As real and inexplicable as their behavior and consequent allegations appeared to the Salem authorites, from our perspective we simply cannot accept the explanation of "demonic possession." As often happens during witch-hunts, the authorities persecuted eccentric, unconventional, and irreligious persons. It has also been argued, by anthropologists Stephen Nissenbaum and Paul Boyer, that the young girls were being used (consciously or unconsciously) by the men to attack certain of their "ungodly" enemies. Thus the victims were women of a certain faction who were ungodly in their pastimes. Whatever the case may be, within six months the girls' moment in the spotlight ended.

There is a striking correspondence between some aspects of the witch trials that we have just analyzed and present-day child-abuse trials. The medieval interrogation methods show similarities to the manner in which young children today are encouraged to disclose their secrets of sexual abuse. A presumed confession is incrementally added to until the full confession (as determined by the interviewers) has been elicited. The leading questions; the refusal to believe anything other than what they want to hear; the drawing from a storehouse of fact, fantasy, and nightmarish theory, leading ultimately to a confession: these are the stock-in-trade methods of today's trained sexual-abuse investigators.

But it is not just the prosecutorial methods of the inquisitors that, though more obviously brutal, seems so uncannily like procedures in modern child-abuse cases. It is the content of the allegations made during the course of the trials: pacts with the devil, riding out to night meetings (during the witch-hunts such rides supposedly took place on broomsticks, whereas today helicopters are used for transportation) for secret revels and sexual orgies, stealing children and eating their flesh. These are millennia-old allegations that pre-date Christianity. They have been levelled by Christians against Jews, by Romans against Christians, by inquisitors against witches, and, in the majority of today's cases, by children against their parents or guardians.

Another strong parallel involves the incentive to implicate friends and neighbors. Today, in the United States, anyone

failing to report someone they suspect of child abuse is subject to a fine. In Canada, mandatory reporting laws apply to
all professionals working with children. Suspicion, in the
lexicon of current child-abuse investigation, is tantamount to
conviction.

Kathleen Morris, the County Attorney presiding over the
Jordan, Minnesota case, offered a deal to James Rud, the
original accused: in return for indicting others, he would get
a light sentence. He accepted. Many of those he accused,
falsely, were similarly encouraged to name other offenders in
return for lighter sentences. By the end of Morris's work with
the Jordan children, they were including more and more
people; many were uttering their nightmarish thoughts to
anyone who would listen; some wanted only to go home and
would lie if necessary to get there. Many other investigators,
following their therapeutic ideology, also encourage suspected molesters to "cop a plea," despite the fact that they
may be innocent. Not all interrogations, of course, lead to the
ultimate disclosure — that is, the ritual sacrifice and murder
of children; however, the admission of guilt is often enough to
satisfy an interrogator or interviewer. But the method practiced in both cases is essentially the same.

Victims of Child Abuse Laws (VOCAL) has chronicled many
cases where accused people, rather than go through with a
public trial and face further disruption of their lives, have
accepted the advice of the investigators and pleaded guilty.
Given the circumstances, they chose to accept the lesser of
two evils and attempt as quickly as possible to pick up the
tattered threads of their family lives. In the worst cases, refusing to plea bargain has landed many in jail, falsely convicted
of child molestation.

The final link between these times of hysteria lies in the
communication of sensationalist stories among a prurient
mass of spectators. We seem willing to believe that the medieval peasants who believed whatever they heard were merely
gullible. Yet today, through national print and broadcast

media, along with highly specialized instructional programs in schools and other institutions, millions of people are hearing about sexual abuse. Front-page descriptions of grotesque rituals involving young children have appeared in every American state and in the larger Canadian cities. Many members of the helping professions are convinced and are convincing others outside their professions that the satanic problem and the attendant sexual abuse that generated concern in the first place are widespread and dangerous. This message is constantly repeated in various forms in various media. Is it surprising, then, that shortly after the first Hamilton trial, two young boys surfaced in the same city (and incidentally, from the care of the same foster mother) with similar tales of horror that they had suffered at the hands of their parents? Or that the famous Jordan, Minnesota, trial was preceded by a flurry of media activity surrounding another alleged satanic abuse case in a nearby town?

Witch confessions, as has been observed by Christina Larner, represented an agreed-upon story between the witch and inquisitor, between the society and God, in which the witch drew, through hallucination or imagination, on a common store of myth, fantasy, and nightmare to respond to the inquisitor's questions.[14]

Today, as in the past, there is an agreement between the laity — the masses — and the psychiatrists and psychologists — the priests of the modern world — about child abuse. Once again we have allegations of satanic practices and once again our panic-stricken response, like that of our European ancestors, is to strike back at our phantasmagoric opponent. Then as now, the problem is that satanists simply do not exist, at least not to the extent that children and our fears lead us to believe.

It is the children's ability to recount explicit tales of sexual abuse that leads many observers to conclude that what they are saying is true. But as with the demoniacs, whose truly bizarre behavior was explained within the context of a religious paradigm, the attempts to explain the strange behavior of children are tenuous at best. What is important, however, is that we can see in retrospect that they were wrong.

It is the belief of present-day legislators that they are right in removing children from their homes, allowing them to be interrogated and drawn, sometimes consciously and more often unconsciously, into accusing their parents or other "significant" persons of sexually abusing them — drawn into the same realm of fantasy that spawned the earlier trials of witches we have briefly explored in this chapter. This tenuous confluence of fantasy and agreed-upon fact, as compelling as it may be, as much as it seems to correspond to events in the world, has not been proven to exist outside the minds of past or present investigators, or the minds of the children into which they consciously or unconsciously tap.

To point out that the unfortunate victims of the Inquisition were forced to confess to what was the fantastic construct of a religiously motivated social order is not to negate the fact that the inquisitors did sometimes find someone who was guilty of some heinous crime. However, the number of innocent people thrown into the hands of the Inquisition numbered in the hundreds of thousands. And today, no one would deny that some children are abused by their parents and other guardians and that we are only now beginning to acknowledge it. Ways must be found to prevent this. But the point here is, how do we deal humanely and justly with the accused? How do we avoid falling into the same "guilt by mere suspicion" pattern that characterized the witch trials? Ideology, however well meant, has a way of blinding one to facts — or fantasies — that stand outside or against one's belief system, and of justifying the most inhuman tactics to deal with them.

The intention of the child-abuse investigators is honest for the most part, stemming from the desire to save innocent children from what they believe to be an intolerable situation.

Such too was the intention of the inquisitors.

5

SADISM:
Sexual Deviance and Psychopathology

It is true that he does not come from a "high risk"
background, and that his psychological and psychiatric
profile does not fit the usual pattern of a person who would
sexually abuse a young child, but as his witness, Dr.
Chamberlain, so eloquently pointed out, sex offenders are
not confined to individuals with certain mental disorders
but include that other group of people known as "normal"
people.

Judge Beckett, Hamilton trial summation, March 30, 1987

Among the confusions that have arisen in the surge of
concern about child abuse can be found the vague equation of the child abuser or molester with the child murderer
and serial murderer. In the area of child abuse, this is a dangerous equation to make, since it is only such distinctions that
will assist legislators, social workers, and the public in their
determinations when a charge of abuse is brought against an
accused person. In this chapter we will examine the characteristics of these deviant personalities in order to reach a fuller
understanding of the types or degrees of deviance.

Child molesters and child murderers are not "normal"
people. Quite the contrary. Research consistently demonstrates that the more aberrant the criminal sexual behavior,
the more disturbed the psychological profile of its perpetrator. This "normal" profile is encapsulated in one of the most
universally used psychological evaluation tools, the Minnesota Multiphasic Personality Inventory (MMPI). Combined

with other methods of assessing individuals — and in the hands of a competent psychologist — the MMPI is a powerful diagnostic indicator. This index demonstrates levels of para-noid, empathic, aggressive, depressive, and other tendencies on a numerical scale. The lower the score or "elevation" in a given area, the closer an individual fits the conventional defi-nition of normal. The child murderer in contrast scores very high in areas that show a tendency toward violence if frus-trated (or even in relatively unstressful times) as well as ten-dencies toward sexual aberrance and depression. Child molesters, on the other hand, form an identifiable group between these two extremes. They are characterized by feel-ings of inadequacy, frustration, and dependency.

Physical violence is very rarely perpetrated by traditional child molesters. Their history is often filled with accounts of loneliness and inadequacy in dealing with adults on an inti-mate level, although they are often successful middle-class citizens. They get their way with children not through threats or violence but through blandishments. Child murderers, on the other hand, seem intent upon physical abuse, torture, and mutilation. They share a history of violent responses to soci-ety from an early age. Their goal is to fulfill a sadistic impulse, and children happen to be their unfortunate victims.

Freund, Heasman, and Roper found that men who pre-ferred sex with young girls or boys — pedophiles — tended to be inadequate, passive, dependent, low in achievement orien-tation, unorganized, insecure, and subservient.[1] Burgess reported a comprehensive study of pedophiles in which ques-tionnaires were sent to 2,383 law-enforcement agencies, of which 832 responded.[2] Pedophiles were primarily interested in sex rings and child pornography. In contrast to the violent depictions of women enjoyed by violent sexual criminals, the pedophiles' pornography, like their crimes, depicted girls and boys fondling and posing naked. Primary access to chil-dren was through occupation, living situation, and other chil-dren. Married men were more often attracted to girls and unmarried men preferred boys. The majority of pedophiles had previous records of sexual offences that ranged from exposing themselves to mutual fondling. Only three subjects reported penetration with victims between the ages of eleven and fourteen. On the whole, they believed that if they had not done physical damage, they had not harmed the child. The researchers found a nearly universal desire among these men to recount their thoughts and experiences, and often they were happy to meet someone to whom they could relate their sexual experiences. In addition, every one of these pedophiles had a collection of child pornography — from a shoebox-full to two truckloads of material — and all maintained files and directories, no matter how much material they possessed.

This composite of the pedophile, supported by researchers such as David Finkelhor, gives a basic picture of the potential or repeat child sexual abuse offender.[3] "That other group of people known as 'normal,' " to whom Judge Beckett referred in his summation, are unlikely candidates for sexually abusing young children in the manner in which the children indicated.

Some studies claim that the main motivation of pedophiles springs from their own abuse as children. Langevin and Lang dispute this theory, having found no significant differences between the early sexual experiences of pedophiles and a "normal" control group. They indicate too that even a history of sexual abuse by itself does not explain enough, since most molested children do not become child abusers in later life.

In an early study by Swenson and Grimes reported by Dr. Ralph Underwager, forty-five nonviolent child sexual abusers, all males, showed pathological MMPI elevations. That is, despite the moderate level of abuse they engaged in — fondling and exhibitionism — their MMPI profiles indicated that they were abnormal.

In contrast to the pedophile, consider the following studies of violent sexual offenders. A study of forty-five men con-victed of sexually abusing children found that among sex offenders in general, the most disturbed MMPI profiles belonged to offenders who committed the more violent sex crimes.[4] Overall, this study suggested that the further the specific sexual behavior of perpetrators moves from the boundaries of acceptable or normal sexual acts, the more pathological such persons' profiles. The study has been repli-cated and confirmed repeatedly, and its findings are borne out in some case studies examined below.

The importance of maintaining a clear distinction be-tween violent and nonviolent offenders is crucial in deter-mining who is likely to commit such a crime. A subject with a normal MMPI profile supported by a battery of other psycho-logical tests and psychiatric assessments, and an incident-free sexual offence history, is an unlikely candidate for sexually exploiting young children. An accused with a normal MMPI profile, who is alleged to have been violently abusive to the point of murdering young children, is an even more highly unlikely candidate for such behavior. While this diagnostic indicator is not infallible, a "normal" reading should gener-ate cautious questioning among investigators searching for the truth of an allegation.

Violence has come to characterize all aspects of the child-abuse debate. One of the primary reasons for this has to do with the increase over the last two decades of a breed of males who commit vicious, sadistic acts against women and occa-sionally children. The FBI, summing up its concern with the rising incidence of violent sexual crime, submitted a report to the Subcommittee on Government Information, Justice and Agriculture in April 1986, which read in part as follows:

> During the last two decades, a new phenomenon appeared in America. That phenomenon we have come to call the serial murderer, a new breed of killer. This

individual is a human predator seeking out his prey to fulfill his fantasy to control and kill. He kills because he is obsessed with killing. He defies our textbooks. He confounds law enforcement by his high degree of mobility. He kills and moves on. . . . In 1966, 12% of the 10,916 murders remained unsolved. Of the 1,130 unsolved, 644 were for no apparent reason. By 1984, 18,692 homicides were reported across the United States. 26% or 5,020 of these homicides remained unsolved. Of the 5,020 unsolved, 4,131 were random, senseless, committed for no apparent reason. There is no way for us to analyze or to estimate how many of those victims were the targets of the repetitive, habitual, serial murderer, but there is a growing concern among us that there is a core of highly skilled habitual killers free in our society. . . . Public pressure is bearing on law enforcement officials throughout our country to take swift and positive measures against serial murderers, serial rapists, child abductors, and child molesters.[5]

(Note the murderer/molester equation appearing now in the police as well as the public mind.)

A breed of man that stalks and hunts women and children? This is a frightening reality. While it is difficult to get a clear statistic on their actual number and their total number of victims, we do know that at least one serial murderer each year is caught and confesses to raping, torturing, and murdering dozens of innocent people, usually women, during his sadistic career. We know too that from 1920 to 1960 an average of two serial killers surfaced every decade. During the 1960s that figure rose to seven. During the 1970s the number climbed to seventeen, and during the 1980s — as of this writing — twenty-seven known serial murderers have been caught.

It is probably no coincidence that at the same time as the number of multiple or serial rapist/murderers began to rise so dramatically, a fledgling radical feminist movement in

North America was gaining converts to its cause. Initially, disparate women's groups articulated an abstract rhetoric attacking the inherent violence of patriarchal systems. By the late 1960s, rape-crisis centers were forming in reponse to the frightening experience of rape, a subject that had been treated until then by social institutions with suspicion, hostility, and silence. Child abuse soon became the focus of the larger concerns of women in an aggressive, male-dominated society.

This development accelerated the organization of child advocates, spawned generous government- and community-supported networks, and made of child abuse a comprehensive and evolving issue that nobody could ignore. But in the process, some facts were obscured. As noted above, child molesters are not violent individuals; they may be exploiting children, they may even be sick and should be treated as such, but they are not in the same league as child murderers. This blurring of distinctions occurs not only in the public mind but also in the courts, where judges, lawyers, and child advocates accuse many "normal" people of this abnormal crime.

The recent linking of child murderer with the child molester reflects the heightened animosity and mistrust we feel for those who have been accused, rightly or wrongly, of sex crimes. This is the problem with trying to come to terms with falsely accused persons in sex-abuse trials. Certain mental-health experts are advising child advocates and the legal system that anyone is capable of these crimes — that, in effect, no one can be trusted. This is precisely the position that Judge Beckett took in declaring that the "normal" psychological profile of one of the accused did not necessarily mean that he hadn't violated the children in his care in unspeakable sexual ways.

The link becomes particularly dangerous in cases of *innocent* people being charged with child sexual abuse. They too are lumped together, in the minds of policemen and the general public, with the sexual murderer. Even in prison, where violence is a way of life, they are considered the lowest form of human being. Yet that kind of atavistic response is not restricted to prison. Consider this statement by the lieutenant-governor of Nevada: "I can sum up my feeling on this sick subject pretty damn quick. Social workers wouldn't like it but you [law enforcement officers] should unstrap that pistol and shoot them on the spot."[6] This level of hatred surrounds all sexual-abuse cases. Such a justifiable fear of male violence, combined with the blurring of distinctions between categories of aberrant behavior, leads investigators to ask whether more grotesque forms of sexual abuse occurred whenever a child or an intermediary reports such an allegation, and to believe the child when he or she gives the information the investigators seek.

As the FBI report on multiple murderers makes clear, murder — and specifically murder committed out of boredom or resentment — is an increasingly common criminal activity in the Western world. Murderers are no longer motivated solely by need or want. Spurred on by an insatiable media that celebrates their existence, by violent pornography — which basically delivers the message to those on the psychological edge that such acts are enjoyable, if not exceedingly reward-ing — and by their all-consuming hatred of society, their numbers can only increase.

While this is an alarming conclusion, it explains the will-ingness of the public to regard the statements of the children in the Hamilton case and others like it — despite the sug-gested level of depravity — as entirely possible, even proba-ble. Child-protection workers, rather than leave a powerless child in the hands of people whom they suspect of abuse, generally err on the side of cautious protection. Accordingly, legislators, rather than err in the face of ambiguous but fright-ening data, similarly favor the alleged victims. Judges, police, parents, psychologists, and psychiatrists become unwitting purveyors of the moral panic generated by the flood of infor-mation telling us about the prevalence of violent sexual crimes, usually committed by men against women and children. This fear, channeled through the issue of child abuse, in many cases turns to outright hysteria and seems justified, despite its damaging effects on those wrongly accused. But if society is going to deal successfully with the damaging consequences of child abuse, we have to become clear about whom and what we are dealing with. What is really at issue here is not that children are being abused, but that a plethora of out-of-context facts and figures distorts our legal and psychological perspectives and leads inevitably to the institutionalization of injustice.

What sets multiple murderers upon their course of human destruction or generates in them compelling sadistic fantasies? How many of them are there? What are they like? The picture of the serial murderer is unpleasant, gruesome, subhuman. Nevertheless, by studying these kinds of murderers we can see exactly what our children are conjuring up in our minds, and in the process gain a finer understanding of why we so easily believe what the children are saying.

Some serial killers, like Charles Manson and the team of Ian Brady and Myra Hindley (better known as the infamous Moors Murderers), tell us that they chose this mode of behavior. All had disturbed childhoods. Even those such as Albert DeSalvo, the Boston Strangler, while shockingly ignorant of their own motives, verge on tragic literature when discussing their lives. One can read volumes about their intent or about who is likely to find inner pain and anger erupting into the calculated frenzy of multiple murder. All of them were severely abused as children, sometimes sexually, sometimes physically, sometimes both. Most were shunted from home to home and many were illegitimate and institutionalized. Indeed, of the twenty-seven serial murderers caught so far this decade, twenty-three had been through the foster-care system — a sobering statistic to consider in light of the tendency to remove children from their allegedly abusive home environments into foster care on the flimsiest of evidence.

Some among them claim that the torture and sexual abuse of their victims are philosophically determined. Very rarely are they delusional, nor do they exhibit any of the classic symptoms of psychiatric disorders, such as incoherence, schizophrenia, or disabling psychosis. Some of them, like Brady, argue that they have the right, even the duty, to go beyond the most sacred of our conventions — the prohibition against the taking of human life. Such thinking loosely follows the writings of the Marquis de Sade, but as yet, the ideology of sadistic murder for pleasure has not been further elaborated.

In many of these cases the multiple murderers choose to act with others; they also generally choose powerless, unknown victims. They maintain that their actions are the actions of free individuals living out a form of the American dream, pursuing life, liberty, and a perverted form of happiness. They use their intelligence in the service of sadomasochistic tendencies. They state openly that they enjoyed what they were doing despite, or perhaps because of, having gone beyond the social conventions that keep most people under control. Many speak of the intense, transient emotional satisfaction they achieve after having committed their premeditated violence.

While it may not convince someone with a developed moral purpose or a sense of the meaning of life, or a clear and prestigious position in the social hierarchy, the nascent "philosophy" of serial murder could easily convince a lonely, frustrated, and abused individual to act out against imagined or actual oppressors. The brutish philosophy, expressed in unambiguously cruel sexual acts, might perhaps call up in his mind his mother who left him, the powerless women he can't meet, the system that has failed him, the young boys who might look up to him if he too could wield such power, or any number of equally obsessive fantasies. To such a person, human beings become objects upon which they can act out what must be a monumental resentment. There are already "hero" serial murderers who have confessed without remorse to their crimes. Many who have been convicted during the last decade named their predecessors as their heroes or simply, without naming anyone else, stated — and this is common — "I just wanted to make a name for myself."

A common trait of serial murderers involves their collecting pornographic literature that depicts violent, degrading acts against women. Feminists, justifiably fighting the pictorial presentations of bondage and sexual violence, have effectively publicized these facts. But the consternation that results has just as effectively led to a panic that sees perversion in every male and generates false accusations. As the number of false accusations rises, a public backlash will develop that will override the insights gained into the lives of abused children. This has already happened in the U.S. And it is beginning to happen in Canada.

Multiple murder in a peaceful social environment is so novel that it requires an entirely new way of thinking on our part to come to terms with it. In the slaughter of innocents in war, or man's perverse exhilaration in the heat of battle, or indeed any brutal action, enjoyment is at least rationalized with ideology. We are not blind to the levels and kinds of violence in the world, to the war cultures that are developing across the Middle East and Third World, to the wanton disregard for human life that has been chronicled in all its mind-numbing forms by groups such as Amnesty International. Given the bleak panorama of human perversity that is broadcast daily by the media, it is difficult not to agree with William Gaylin, the American psychiatrist who has written about multiple murder, when he states that all of us in our unconscious are "killers, rapists, incestual, exhibitionistic, voyeuristic, aggressive, and homicidal."[7] But for most of us these urges remain locked in the unconscious.

What has happened to North America during the latter half of this century that has caused these primeval urges to dominate the consciousness of a growing number of men? It requires a radical shift of the mind to directly confront this evil among us.

One of the earliest and only surviving accounts of a multiple murderer concerns Gilles de Rais, the infamous fifteenth-century French baron who fulfilled his perverse pleasures by sexually abusing and torturing some 130 peasant children. But Gilles de Rais proved to be more a forerunner of things to come than a representative of things as they were. Until the last century, only about a dozen such individuals had been caught and had confessed the extent of their pathological hatred.

In the early years of this century, North American criminals who murdered generally did so in gang wars or while robbing banks. The heroes among criminals were the likes of Al Capone or Bonnie and Clyde. Despite their calculated ability to kill, these criminals did so for specific gains: wealth, power, territory, and so on. Their victims had something that the gangsters wanted, something that they were willing to overstep the bounds of conventional morality to obtain. This criminological fact remained relatively constant in North America until the latter half of this century.

It is not surprising that many of these apparently motiveless crimes take place in sunny California, where mental and physical overcrowding is the norm. Thousands of men and women wander down to California from across the States, creating what one researcher has called a "behavioral toilet." Similarly, serial murderers' presence is notable in and around New York, Miami, Houston, Washington. They tend to stake out a wide territory as their "hunting" ground. Some, like Ted Bundy and Charles Ng, make forays into Canada, where their venues tend to be largely Toronto, and to a lesser degree Vancouver, (the home of Clifford Olson, Canada's most notorious sex murderer). Canada lags behind the United States in population density and in the number of homicides, though this number too can be expected to change. In 1987, approximately one hundred Toronto men were charged with serial rape, murder, or some other violent sexual crime. At present, Canadian men who feel the urge for violent sex are more prone, it seems, to become serial rapists than murderers.

In 1956, Jack Henry Abbott was sent to jail. He was twelve years of age. Over the next thirty-three years he was only out of jail for five months. In prison he read the works of philosophers and social thinkers and became, in his mind anyway, a Marxist. He began corresponding with Norman Mailer, who was so impressed with the intensity of Abbott's voice that he persuaded Random House to publish a selection of the letters under the title *In the Belly of the Beast*. In essence, the book romanticized the "necessary" act of violence. Some lines in the book are chilling: "Dangerous killers who act alone and without emotion, who act with calculation and principles, with acts of murder.... This is a man." The book was an immediate best-seller, not simply because Mailer had pressed for its release but also because it stated something to a bored segment of the population who perhaps needed a pseudo-aesthetic justification for violence and acts of murder.

On the strength of Mailer's intervention, Abbott was released from jail. Within six months he had murdered a twenty-year-old waiter who had informed him that he could not use a restaurant's staff washroom. There was nothing romantic or "necessary" about this murder, but it points to a type of intellectually justified criminality that seems to be on the increase. Abbott tried to justify it with incoherent references to Nietzsche and other philosophers. The ideologues of Nazism had done the same. Abbott, though he did not indulge his fantasy of necessary murder on a serial basis, nevertheless articulated a philosophy of killing for its own sake.

Ian Brady and Myra Hindley span the gap between rational justification and the bored, resentful sex murderer whose passion for bloody murder or sex or both cannot be restrained by either social norm or moral taboo.

Brady was the bastard son of a Scottish waitress; he never knew his father. He was raised in Gorbal, the roughest slum district in Glasgow, where he was known for his penchant for torturing other children and maiming animals. Brady grew up thin, pale, homosexually oriented — a misfit. He was a drunkard, a petty criminal, and an avid reader. His library contained over thirty instructive titles, including *The History of Torture through the Ages*, *Sex Crimes and Sex Criminals*, *The Life and Ideas of the Marquis de Sade*, *The Kiss of the Whip*, *Sexual Anomalies and Perversions*, and *Nuremberg Diary*. He also read *Mein Kampf* in the original German. Brady followed the philosophy of the Marquis de Sade and Gilles de Rais, both of whom by word and act propounded that freedom consists in taking whatever gives one pleasure. Brady was specifically entranced by the Nazi slaughter of the Jews and by violent pornography.

His companion, Myra Hindley, whom he affectionately referred to as Myra Hess, was a dim-witted secretary who met Brady at the office where they both worked for a brief time. They flouted all conventions. They posed for pornographic pictures in full sadomasochistic attire; both wore chains and leather and carried whips. Hindley dressed like Irma Grese, the Nazi concentration camp guard and sadist who became known to the British army of occupation after the Second World War as "the Female Beast of Belsen." They contemplated armed robbery as a way of making money and outraging the authorities. Instead they decided on murder.

Together these two people abducted, sexually molested, and tortured young boys and girls from Manchester and surrounding areas. Afterwards, they killed their victims and buried them on the moors. Their greatest kick while committing these acts was to tape-record their victims' screams and pleas for mercy as they were subjected to hideously painful torture. Later Brady and Hindley listened to the tapes and viewed photographs they had taken, and thereby achieved orgasm.

They also posed for the camera on the graves of their child victims. Nobody is quite certain how many they killed, although at least eight young people disappeared during their reign of terror.

Myra Hindley made international headlines in October 1986 when she tried to convince the authorities that she was ready to be paroled, after serving twenty years of her sentence. There was an immediate outcry. She hastened to assure the public that she had changed drastically, and as a measure of good faith was willing to show the police where they had buried the bodies. One of the victims' parents stated quite unequivocally to the press that "if she [got] out [he would] hunt her down and kill her with a knife." In July 1987, Myra Hindley informed the police where the bodies were buried on the moors, and the bodies were recovered. Myra Hindley is still in jail.

Could anybody have guessed at the strange couple's predilection for violence and sex? Probably not, at least not without the results of extensive psychological testing. Despite the clues — the disturbed childhood, the revealing library, and so on — until they acted out their privately held dual fantasies they were simply two strange people in love. And even then, these two people worked in offices and went about their daily lives without suspicion during a three-year rampage that saw at least eight children murdered.

This unsettling, somewhat puzzling, theme — that such people are superficially unrecognizable, that they could be anybody — will come up again and again as we meet others of these types. Although such observations break down under close scrutiny, this theme still weaves uneasily through the body politic that they are attacking.

It should be noted here that sexual murderers, after they are caught, find it difficult, if not impossible, to obscure their motives or fantasies. While they may refuse to admit to the crime (though this is uncommon), they will very often lead investigators to damning pieces of evidence that will finally, irrevocably indict them. This nearly universal confessional trait of serial murderers differs strikingly from the present spate of alleged satanic child sexual murders. Despite the hundreds of children making these allegations and despite the multitude of cases that have come before the courts or to the attention of health-care professionals, few of the accused fit the known characteristics of violent abusers, few confess, and no evidence has been found to substantiate the claims of their accusers. It is especially remarkable in the Hamilton case, where the level of brutality and sexual exploitation is equal — if we accept the allegations of the children — to that in the moors murders. This alone should give us pause when prosecuting or intervening in the lives of individuals accused of these kinds of crimes. Even in the case of seemingly normal persons charged with serious sex crimes, material evidence is the final factor that distinguishes them from the rest of society. Such criminals leave an undeniable trail of blood and mutilated bodies in their wake.

Between 1974 and 1978 a witty, articulate, handsome young student stalked across America hunting down, sexually assaulting, and sadistically murdering women. Yet people who had known him for decades, as well as people who met him through the investigation, felt initially that his being charged must have been a mistake.

A search of his room turned up nothing incriminating. He was a psychology student, active in local politics, well liked by both his peers and his teachers. However, when his photograph was identified by a number of women, he was charged with murder.

Ted Bundy became a model prisoner. He was good-natured, good-looking, and well-educated. His parents — intelligent, respectable members of the middle class — supported him to the hilt. Even the prison guards believed that Bundy couldn't be a multiple sex killer. He acted as his own lawyer, studied law, ate vegetarian meals at his request (he couldn't stand the thought of killing animals, he said). Before long he was making court appearances without manacles. But while he didn't seem like the kind who could commit multiple sex murders, evidence against him mounted quickly. He was identified by victims whom he had tried to abduct, and his credit card receipts showed that he had been in the areas where certain of the young women had been killed.

Bundy — because he needed to kill some more young women, because it was impossible for him to control his urge to kill — escaped from prison by hacking his way through a window. He ended up in Tallahassee, Florida where, on January 15, 1978, two weeks after escaping from jail and four years after starting on his murderous rampage, he attacked and almost killed another woman.

Even in the final days of Bundy's trial, when the packed courtroom looked with sympathy at the man who refused to admit his guilt — despite his toothmarks being found on one of the victim's buttocks — no one could understand how this man, a man with promise and potential, could have chosen this sordid path.

This is precisely the twentieth-century crime, the kind of crime we have been encountering more and more in recent years. This kind of violence — calculated, explosive, unmotivated, and vicious — is becoming the norm rather than the exception. These murderers may appear every bit as capable as most other people; and except for this maddening desire, this urge that both terrifies and exhilarates them, they *are* normal. But only on the surface. Under the intense scrutiny of the law, psychiatry, and psychology, their façades break down. And the evidence against them, often their own, is always weighty.

Bundy spoke of a malignant being inside him that gradually dominated his consciousness and made violent rape and murder a necessity. This gruesome obsession, according to FBI interviews, is common to mass murderers.

Around the same time that Bundy was beginning his spree,

the police arrived at Dean Allen Corll's Dallas house on an August evening. Corll was lying naked, splattered in blood and loose pieces of flesh where bullets had pierced his now-lifeless body. Three frightened teenagers, two boys and a girl, huddled outside the front door. One of the boys, Wayne Henley, had earlier phoned the police and admitted to the killing, and now handed over the murder weapon. Then the frightened Henley told his nightmarish story.

Corll, a homosexual, had become enraged when Henley brought a girl (along with another boy) to the house. After sniffing acrylic paint, a common practice with Corll, all three youths had fallen asleep on the floor. When Henley woke up he was tied and handcuffed, and Corll was threatening to kill him. Henley "sweet-talked" Corll into letting him go. He had to promise, though, to rape and kill the girl while Corll did the same to the boy. Henley agreed, but once freed he picked up the gun and fired on the taunting Corll, killing him.

Henley told the police that he had procured boys for Corll at $200 each and knew that Corll had killed a number of them. He took the police to boathouses where they dug up more than thirty bodies. As it turned out, Henley, a young friend called Brooks, and Corll had each actively engaged in murdering and torturing young male victims. Corll would often keep the boys for several days and perform various sexual acts with them on his specially constructed plywood board.

Both Henley and Brooks — uneducated, impoverished, and inarticulate — received life sentences. From what could be reconstructed of Corll's life, he had had an unhappy childhood, spent mostly with his divorced mother. During his earliest years, his father had beaten him mercilessly for every misdemeanor. He spent a few years in the army before drifting to Dallas to live near his mother. At about thirty years of age he began to hang around with youths whom he would pay to have sex with him; he organized glue-sniffing parties, presumably to get the boys high before seducing them. What pushed him over the edge or what kind of fantasy life forced him into his gory pastime can only be guessed at, but in most respects Corll is a commonplace figure among twentieth-century sex murderers.

Henley and Brooks stated at the time that at first they were "just in it for the good times but then it kinda got crazy." What good times? And at what number of dead bodies did they decide that it was getting "kinda crazy"? Other adolescents with the same brutish intelligence would express similar comments to police and psychologists over the next few years.

Melvin Davis Reese was a jazz musician who played piano, guitar, saxophone, and clarinet. People who had worked with him described him as mild-mannered and intelligent.

Early one summer evening a black man approached an army sergeant and his girlfriend who were sitting in a car on a lonely sideroad near an abandoned farm. He explained that he was the care-taker of the property, asked for a light, then pulled out a gun and climbed into the back seat. He grabbed Margaret Harold's hair, pulled her head backward, and demanded money. "Don't give it to him," Margaret Harold spit out. A shot rang out in the darkness and Harold slumped forward in her seat. The sergeant jumped from the car and ran to a nearby farmhouse, where he phoned the police. When they arrived a short time later, Harold's body was still slumped over, but the corpse had been violated.

Police came across a shack in a clearing not far from the scene of the gruesome murder. Inside, the walls were covered with pornographic photographs and police morgue shots of women who had been murdered. The shack belonged to Melvin Reese. Although the evidence was all too damning, Reese's musician friends refused to believe it.

In his diaries Reese had written: "Caught them on a lonely road. . . . Drove to a select area and killed husband and baby. Now the mother and daughter were all mine." He went on to describe the perversions he forced upon the mother before he killed her and turned to her frightened daughter, writing,

"Now I was her master." He then described in detail how he mutilated her and enjoyed watching her slowly and painfully die.

Reese, like many we have encountered so far, was a hardened killer who was satisfied only when a woman lay stretched out dead and mutilated before him. He felt no remorse. Despite his general level of competence and seeming sincerity, his home and the trail behind him were littered with emblems of his sadistic passion. Material evidence.

"Normal" people do not do such things.

Like terrorists, multiple murderers are sensational and violent facts of modern life. Their stories sell newspapers and lift sagging network ratings. They appear on the cover of *Time* magazine and receive careful consideration in the *Christian Science Monitor*. When both Phil Donahue and Oprah Winfrey host shows on satanism and sexuality revolving around these chilling issues, you know that they have touched upon a very large sore spot in public awareness.

The powerful capacity of the media to both reveal and fuel the mind-numbing fears that these kinds of people generate cannot be underestimated. Some mass murderers, like terrorists, are extremely sophisticated in their use of the media. Consider the case of the Zodiac killer of San Francisco, California. Between December 1968 and October 1969, the Zodiac murdered five people and left two severely wounded. Nobody is certain how many more deaths he was responsible for, although in his last known correspondence with the police, he claimed that he had killed over thirty people.

Two bodies were found on a lovers' lane just outside San Francisco. A teenager, David Farraway, lay beside the right wheel of his car, a bullet hole behind his left ear. Betty Lou Jensen was sprawled in the grass, face down, with several bullet holes in her back. There appeared to be no motive for the killings: the young man's wallet was untouched and the woman had not been sexually assaulted.

Approximately six months later, the Vallejo police department received a call from a gruff-voiced man who spat out abruptly, "If you will go one mile east on Columbus Parkway to a public park, you will find the kids in a brown car. They have been shot with a 9-mm Luger. I also killed those kids last year. Goodbye." Arriving at the scene, the police found Michael Mageau, barely alive, and beside him, dead, Darlene Ferrin, mother of a young child. Mageau informed the police that a stocky man had come up to the car, blinded them with a flashlight, walked over to the side, and without a word had begun shooting them. Shortly after that the *Vallejo Times-Herald* received letters signed with a cross over a circle, a sign of the zodiac. The descriptions of the murder in the letters convinced the police that they were authentic communications from the killer. The Zodiac, as he came to be called, warned that he would "go on a rampage" if his letters were not published. The newspaper published the letters. The police found no clue to the killer's identity.

Some weeks later, the police received a phone call telling them details of the previous murder as well as one just committed. Police found a taxi driver lying dead beside his car.

San Franciscans were terrified. Thousands of leads followed every murder. The police had a number of clues, including a description, the voice, even three fingerprints that they had found on a pay telephone to which they had traced one of the calls: but the clues led nowhere. In a letter to the *San Francisco Chronicle*, the Zodiac complained of, among other things, the bungling police efforts. He concluded: "School children make nice targets. I think I shall wipe out a school bus some morning. Just shoot the tires, then pick off the kiddies as they come bouncing out."

Three weeks later, on October 21, Zodiac informed the Oakland police station that he would be willing to give himself up if he could be defended by F. Lee Bailey, the high-profile criminal lawyer, and Melvin Belli. He also demanded time on a popular early-morning talk show. It was arranged, and thousands of people anxiously tuned in to the Jim Dunbar Show at 6:45 one morning. At 7:41 their vigil was rewarded with a soft, boyish voice complaining about his headaches and the murders. He hung up, but called back fifteen times, at one point talking with Melvin Belli. He signed off after arranging to meet Belli in front of a store in Daly City, but he failed to turn up.

In 1971 the *Los Angeles Times* received a letter complaining about the lack of police effort and concluding with: "The reason I am writing to the *Times* is this, they don't bury me on the back pages like the others." The Zodiac remains unidentified.

The Zodiac, who in many ways resembles the better-known Son of Sam (Berkowitz), demonstrates the tremendous importance of the media/murderer relationship. For one full year Californians in general, and San Franciscans in particular, were kept in something resembling a state of siege — largely through constant media coverage, that the Zodiac exploited. The killer was at large; he could have been anybody, and he could have struck anywhere. And as if that were not enough, the presence of another, equally inspired, sadistic murderer heightened this state of panic.

While the *Vallejo Times-Herald* was publishing the Zodiac's letters announcing that he "[liked] killing people because it [was] so much fun," Charles Manson was sending his LSD-tripping murderers to the home of Sharon Tate. On August 8, 1969, just two weeks after the Zodiac's second motiveless murder, Susan Atkins, one of Manson's "girls," stood over the mutilated body of Sharon Tate, dipped a towel in her blood and scrawled "pig" on the floor.

The Zodiac remained an intensely disturbing figure, but the shockwaves that emanated from his crimes were strictly local. Manson, however, achieved international status by murdering famous people in a sensational fashion, by his grandstanding courtroom tactics, and by a sophisticated manipulation of the media through which he showed us the dark side of human nature. In many ways Manson has become a screen behind which we keep the more puzzling and disturbing aspects of sexual sadism.

Manson came from a broken home; he was a misfit, an outcast who (given the chance) might have been different. In some ways, though we can never approve of his deeds, we can respond — if only ambiguously — to the guilt trip that Manson consciously laid on Americans. "You did this to me," he said to the sociologists and psychiatrists. "You did this to my girls," he said to middle-class mothers and fathers across America. "You can do the same thing I've done," he said to hundreds of thousands of kids whose lives had been shattered, an indirect leader to them just as he was to his community of middle-class adolescents. In a strange way he became a counter-culture hero. He articulated a troubled American youth's resentment, and he mixed his manic insight with murder. But whether we understand Manson as a victim of society, wounded into depravity, or a simple must-be-locked-up psychopath loosely identified with satanism, he holds a unique position in the history of North American criminality, for he forced us to face the presence of distinctly modern murderers in our midst. And each one who surfaced after Manson etched that awful truth just one notch deeper into our collective psyche.

The general public is bringing great pressure to bear on governments, law-enforcement agencies, and educators to remove from society this kind of violence, no matter how rooted it may be in sickness. Unfortunately, this kind of murderer generates unwarranted fears in those who deal with child-abuse issues.

An essential discovery has been made in studying the modern multiple murderer, buttressed by the confessions of the most sexually violent men: *severe* abuse in childhood, sexual and otherwise, produces profoundly disturbed adults. But social workers and child advocates are applying this frightening knowledge to the complex of issues surrounding child abuse in a way that feeds hysteria. For people like Manson and Bundy represent rare and highly exceptional aberrations. In reality, a much smaller proportion of children are actually abused than members of the helping professions would have us believe — and of this number, only an infinitesimally small percentage are so severely abused as to be in danger of becoming multiple murderers.

Manson's claim — now supported by research evidence — that society collectively "did this to [him]" leaves us both guilty and enlightened. In our laudable efforts, however, to prevent the kind of severe abuse that produces a man like this, we cast our net too wide, consuming precious resources of energy and funding with programs aimed at an inflated population of abused children that exists only in our terrified imagination.

This is what the crimes of the twentieth century have brought us to: sex, murder, children and women entangled in a network of frightening social and psychic dimensions. And in the issue of child sexual abuse we are faced with the tremendous task of understanding how we can alleviate the abundance of nightmarishly violent sexual imagery that has seeped into the minds of young children, an imagery invoked by the thoughts of Albert DeSalvo, known as the Boston Strangler, as he reflects on his early years:

> We didn't have to do anything to get beaten, just be around when the old man was ready to hand out the beatings. I saw my father knock my mother's teeth out and then break every one of her fingers. . . . I must have been seven. Ma was laid out under the sink — I watched it. . . . He once sold my sister and me into slavery for nine dollars, sold us to some farmer in Maine. No one knew what happened to us. For six months Ma hunted for us and couldn't find us.

But we would take off over to Eastie, Noodle Island,

and hide out under the piers and he would be afraid to come looking for us there because the other kids living there would've helped us kill him just for the couple of bucks they might get off his body. . . . You know, that was a dangerous place. They was kids with no home at all. That was where they lived — under the piers and in the old warehouses and wharves. They was wharf rats, that's what people called them and they was just like rats — and they was a million real rats there, too, big ones that wasn't afraid of you — those kids, those wharf rats, I saw them roll a drunk one night, landing on him the way the real rats would land on one of their own kind who was sick or hurt all in a big dirty, wiggling pile, ripping and tearing until the thing that they was on was dead and eaten to the bones. . . . Them kids was small, some of them wasn't more than ten, eleven, but they was a lot of them and they got that drunk down, just like the real rats, and they practically tore him to pieces then dumped his body into the water. Nothing happened to them, bodies was always being fished out of the harbor all beat up and fish-eaten.[8]

DeSalvo's pitiful history elicits a flood of sympathy for the man who brutally murdered thirteen women and allegedly raped nearly a thousand. He took no thought for their lives, nor for their families. Although we cannot exonerate him or the breed of being he represents, his savage childhood does show how essential it is to stop the abuse of all children. In court DeSalvo was asked by his lawyer if he desired further psychiatric treatment. He answered: "What I always asked for was medical help, and I haven't received any."

Albert DeSalvo inadvertently and eloquently argues for the same thing that child-abuse investigators have been fighting for in the past decade. Our realizations about the repercussions of abuse in childhood have given rise to the dilemma that this book has been dealing with: our intense desire to rescue children from abuse has prompted us to hastily remove children from their homes whenever there is the slightest hint of possible abuse. But not all abused children are severely or seriously enough abused to warrant state intervention. State intervention and institutional care for children have their own hazards, as Chapter 2 showed. Finding the balance between protection of children and protection of innocent parents is the challenge that must be faced. Otherwise, "normal" people will be scapegoated, the children who are indeed abused and in need of our help will remain unassisted, and those who are not will be abused in another sense by the very institutions that are purportedly set up to serve and to save them.

6
CHILDHOOD:
The Roots of Violence

Sadism is not an infectious disease that strikes a person all of a sudden. It has a long prehistory in childhood and always originates in the desperate fantasies of a child who is searching for a way out of a hopeless situation.
Alice Miller, *For Your Own Good*, 1983

Child abuse is not a new problem. As our brief survey of the paradigms of childhood revealed, the history of child abuse is long and insufferably ugly. Indeed, the further back one goes, as psychohistorian Lloyd de Mause has demonstrated, "the more likely children are to [have been] beaten, terrorized, abandoned, sexually abused, and killed as a matter of course." And if it is true, as Wordsworth wrote, that "the child is father to the man," then it is little wonder that abuse has been perpetuated from generation to generation. Violence is a nightmare from which children, though they play different roles when adults, never fully recover.

This chapter examines the organic link between the experiences of childhood and the behavior of an adult. It begins by chronicling the routine measures that were once taken by educators and parents to repress childhood initiative, curiosity, and other unwanted traits in order to raise what were, according to the standards of the day, "good" children. Given that we are dealing primarily with a period of history (the fifteenth through twentieth centuries) in which religious principles dominated social and intellectual life, it is natural that religious and moralistic ideals frequently emerge as the good intentions that pave the way to hell. But the real villains — or, more precisely, victims — are the parents, who project their unmet needs onto what they perceive as their wayward charges, battering them into submission "for their own good," and causing them in turn to become equally terrifying victim/villains as they go on to re-enact their childhood traumas.

Despite some uncertainty about what defines child abuse today, and despite the variance across time and cultures in the meaning of childhood abuse, there is no mistaking what is meant by abuse in this chapter. The practices described appear to us as obvious and depressingly deliberate abuses.

In the early-modern period of Western history, abuse was the common expression of the child–parent relationship. Even sexual abuse, recognized today as an experience capable of turning children into violent psychopaths or multiple personalities, was an everyday matter for children in most of Western Europe until the late nineteenth century. This may partly explain the morbid fascination so common in that period with the ingeniously perverse tortures reserved for common criminals and heretics — public hangings, beheadings, and drawing-and-quarterings. These "recreations" were enjoyed by the clergy, politicians, and the public, and continued unabated in most of Western Europe, as did common forms of child abuse, until so recently in our history.

Philippe Ariès, whose studies of European notions of sexuality and death are properly regarded as definitive, came up with so many vivid and varied examples of child–parent sexual relations that he was led to conclude that "playing with children's privy parts formed part of a widespread tradition." Anna Burr studied 250 autobiographies from this period and concluded that not one of them revealed happy memories of childhood. J. Louise Despert's *The Emotionally Disturbed Child, Then and Now* relentlessly pursues the evidence of mistreatment that children have routinely suffered in Western culture since antiquity. Toward the end of her study, she expresses her growing horror over such "unremitting heartlessness and cruelty."[1]

Today there are a number of post-Freudians whose recent

works, albeit significantly diverging from their mentor's, are consistent with the facts of childhood abuse. Following Lloyd de Mause and Alice Miller, a psychohistorian and psychoanalyst respectively, my premise here — as just stated — is that the child is the inheritor of the unconscious, unmet needs and desires of the parent. That is, the adult projects onto the child all the unconscious psychic disturbances from which he or she suffers; the child, in turn, unconsciously acts out these same projections with his or her children. The sins of the fathers are quite literally visited upon the sons.

In the model, the family is the basic unit within which socialization occurs, within which children's development is monitored and retarded, nurtured, or otherwise directed. Children, at first powerless under the parents' constant surveillance and punishment-and-reward system, gradually learn how to acquire some control over their surroundings. The ability to express or repress love and the other intense emotions of childhood, the capacity for learning, the ways of assigning values to objects and ideas — all these are learned during the first few years of life and pave the way to adult development.

Throughout this socialization process, children are taught to respect and love the all-powerful adults, who mould children in their own image. To successfully fulfill the demands of the parents, no matter how disabling or sadistic or traumatic, and at the same time maintain love and respect for them, children repress those thoughts and feelings that seem to conflict with their assigned roles. This is the origin of what Freud called the "repetition compulsion" phenomenon. Unable to understand or grasp their parents' unloving commands, children, for their own psychic equilibrium, repress both the knowledge of and the natural responses to those unkind acts.

By the time children reach adolescence, they have learned to repress those thoughts and feelings that were unacceptable to parents and society. Yet however strongly those acts are repressed, their impact remains in the psyche and finds release in the commission of secret, frequently neurotic or perverse, acts.

This is especially true following puberty, when powerful sexual urges rise to the surface and bring with them a complex of intense feelings. It requires all the energy at one's disposal to keep those feelings repressed; to maintain control is, after all, absolutely essential to "getting along" in society. To lose control is to unleash all the rage and hostility that has been pent up in the unconscious since the suffering of those early traumas. And the unleashing is not a random impulse but is in direct proportion to the kind and amount of rage the person felt during those long-forgotten traumas.

Admittedly, this is a theoretical model, and as such it is debatable. However, the historian of childhood must inevitably conclude that the evolution of child-rearing practices is characterized by "unreasonable fears, folklore, fanaticism, medical and physical sadism, and gross abuse and misuse of parental authority,"[2] which in most cases appear to be detrimental to the child's and ultimately the adult's psychological health.

It is comforting to know that the child-abuse practices described below, which are typical of early-modern child-rearing practices, though they continue, are no longer officially sanctioned.

This first account, written by a young German, recalls a scene from his childhood, in 1739.

> "Nicolas, your father loves you; do you love him?"
> "Yes, Grandpapa!"
> "Suppose you were in danger and to save yourself it was necessary to put your hand in the fire, would you do it? Would you put it there if it was necessary?"
> "Yes, Grandpapa."
> "And for me?"

"For you, yes, yes."

"And for your father? For you mamma?"

"Both of them, both of them!"

"We shall see if you are telling the truth, for your mother is in great need of your little help. If you love her, you must prove it."

I made no answer; but putting together all that had been said, I went to the fireplace and, while they were making signs to each other, put my right hand into the fire. The pain drew a deep sigh from me.[3]

Rather than being aberrant behavior for this period, this was a common, and comparatively gentle, example of early-modern child-rearing practices. To ensure that children were properly socialized, the Dr. Spocks of Renaissance Europe unanimously recommended many brutal forms of physical and psychological punishment, such as severe beating, leaving children in cold, dark places, and when they became intolerable, hanging them in unnatural positions. In many of these examples, the onus is on the children to prove themselves, or their love, to the parents, and the required proof is often highly destructive.

An American father in 1830 tells of horsewhipping his four-year-old son because the boy could not read. He tied up the naked boy in the cellar.

With him in this condition, and myself, the wife of my bosom and the lady of my family, all of us in distress and with hearts sinking within us, I commenced using the rod. During this most unpleasant, self-denying and disagreeable work, I made frequent stops, commanding and trying to persuade, silencing excuses, answering objections. . . . I felt all the force of divine authority and express command that I ever felt in any case in all my life. . . . But under the all-controlling influence of such a degree of angry passion and obstinacy, as my son had manifested, no wonder he thought he "should beat me

out" knowing as he did that it made me feeble and
tremulous as I was. At that time he could neither pity me
nor himself.[4]

Let's follow that interaction for a moment, looking at it
through the eyes of an empathetic spectator. The child is four
years old. He is naked, tied to a chair in a cold, dark cellar. He
is afraid and powerless. His crime? He can't read. His punishment? To be beaten mercilessly by what would appear to be an
insanely angry father, so pitched with enthusiasm for his task
that he feels it may be "divine authority" that guides him. He
says his act is "self-denying and disagreeable" and that his
obstinate, four-year-old, illiterate son tied naked to the chair is
trying to "beat him out" (that is, outwit him). This is a primary
example of what psychiatrists call projection, which until
recently was one of the most disturbing yet stable aspects of
the child–parent relationship.

If this were an isolated account, we could pass it off as the
relationship of a madman to his son. But it is not. Both these
accounts are taken from Lloyd de Mause's seminal study, *The
History of Childhood*. In hundreds of examples, de Mause demonstrates utterly shameless acts perpetrated against children
and defended by pedagogues, along with horrifying practices
that were so commonly enacted by parents and teachers of
this period that it was not deemed necessary to defend them.
We encounter in such incidents a way of thinking so distant
from our own that it might as well belong to another planet.

In the case of the American father, note the quasi-religious
enthusiasm with which he undertakes his task. Often during
this period torture is intimately associated with religious
sentiment bordering on the mystical. There are several reasons for this. Christianity has at its root the two great mythic
images of Western culture: the image of the Suffering One,
Christ crucified, hands and feet nailed to a cross and thorns
across his brow, and the image of Jehovah himself driving the
sinful Adam and Eve from the paradisal garden. The message
of these two profound images is that life is suffering and that

at the root of our souls we are evil because of Adam's fall: "The new born babe is full of the stains and pollution of sin, which it inherited from our first parents through our loins."[5]

The German writer Christoph Meckel recognized this powerful blending of God, father, and suffering in his own upbringing. Writing in his autobiography of the type and severity of his father's beatings, he says:

> Whatever it was that happened in Paradise involving Adam, Eve, the serpent, and the apple, the well-deserved Biblical thunderbolt of prehistoric times, the roar of the Almighty and His pointed finger signifying explusion — I know nothing about all that. It was my father who drove me out of Paradise.[6]

Although the particular methods of "discipline" varied, the intent was uniform: childhood was something from which to escape, a state lacking both God-given grace and social refinement. Children were thought to be so "full of the devil" that children's stories contained detailed accounts of the tortures God had in store for them in hell if they didn't conform. "The child is in this red-hot oven. Hear how it screams to come out."[7] In *A Godly Form of Household*, an influential child-rearing manual of the sixteenth century, Robert Cleaver wrote: "The young child which lieth in the cradle is both wayward and full of affections; and though his body be but small, yet he hath a wrong doing heart, and is altogether inclined towards evil." Many children among the well-to-do classes were given as many as a thousand enemas to flush evil from their bodies. Cotton Mather, a leading Salem clergyman at the time of the witch-hunts, conveyed the same message in his sermons and to his own daughters. "I took my little daughter, Katy, into my Study; and there I told my Child that I am to dy shortly. . . . I sett before her, the sinful and woful Condition of her Nature, and charged her to prey in secret places, without ceasing that God for the sake of Jesus Christ would give her a New Heart, and pardon Her Sins."[8] There are two points to stress here: his daughter was a mere eight years old, and Mather was not going to die.

Even when religion slipped into the psychological background of the child–parent relationship, everyday morality lessons still bordered on the cruel, grotesque, and bizarre. For instance, to strengthen their moral resolve children were taken out of school to attend public hangings. As well, parents took their children to the local gibbet to see the bodies and then, when they returned home, whipped them to "instill in their memory what they had seen."[9] The effect that such "lessons" must have had on impressionable prepubescent children is almost too gruesome to imagine. The following is a case in point.

In the mid-seventeenth century, Harriet Spencer, an eleven-year-old girl, was taken by her father to view hundreds of decomposing corpses. Her father felt that it was time for Harriet to overcome her superstitions and fears of the dead, and he conscientiously espoused contemporary theories of child development, no doubt with the best of intentions. Harriet writes in her diary:

> I followed him down a dark narrow steep staircase that wound round and round a long way till they opened a door into a great cavern. It was lit by a lamp hanging down in the middle, and [there was] a friar, carrying a torch in his hand. At first I could not see, and when I could I hardly dared look, for on every side there were horrid black ghastly figures, some grinning, pointing at us, or seeming in pain, in all sorts of postures, and so horrid I could hardly help screaming, and I thought they all moved. When Papa saw how uncomfortable I was, he was not angry but very kind, and said I must conquer it and go and touch one of them, which was very shocking. Their skin was all dark brown and quite dried up on the bones, and quite hard and felt like marble.[10]

This is a remarkable contrast to the father who tied his

child to a chair and whipped him for his own good, though the lesson for both children is a cruel one. Harriet's father is concerned for her psychological well-being. He is kindly in his approaches to her. He is what we today would call a concerned parent. Yet today we look at the teaching and ask what could possibly be learned by seeing and touching decomposing corpses. A full century later, forcing young children to contemplate dead bodies was encouraged as a way of teaching them about sex "without exciting their passions unduly." The reality for early-modern parents across Europe was to abuse their children — in good faith, perhaps, but in a terribly misguided way.

One of the most detailed accounts of childhood during the early-modern period is found in the diary of Heroard, doctor and biographer of Louis XIII. The brief scene recounted below reveals ideas about childhood common to all classes at that time. Control of the child was paramount, and children were wrapped in swaddling bandages and left motionless for many hours at a time, day after day, month after month (more on this later). The control was not for the child's sake but was rather for the convenience of the parents or nurse. Among the upper classes this form of control, because less influenced by necessity, was more subtle and sometimes even playful. Quite often children would be put on a leash like a dog or be manipulated with strings like a puppet, the playthings of their parents or guardians. What is interesting in the following case is that the child becomes a fully eroticized being in the minds of the adults around him (or at least for Heroard).

Heroard describes the one-year-old dauphin "lifting up his skirt to show him his cock. . . . He makes everyone kiss his cock. . . . In the company of the little girls, he pulls up his skirt, and shows her his cock with such ardor that he is completely beside himself." He recounts that the dauphin is so excited that he "makes his women come, makes them dance, plays with the little Marguerite, kisses her, embraces her, throws her down and casts himself upon her with quivering body, and grinding teeth. . . . He strives to hit her on the buttocks with a birch rod."

The story is told as if the sexually precocious king-to-be is simply being watched by his delighted elders, though in fact members of the royal household are manipulating his actions with strings. Heroard tells us that Louis XIII, between one and seven years of age, developed intimate sexual liaisons with the King, the Queen, or both together in their bed, and kept a bevy of servants sexually satisfied. However, at the age of nine he was compelled to denounce the flesh as sinful and to never again publicly mention his "privy parts." To strengthen him in this resolve, he was whipped each morning upon awakening; the resulting nightmares plagued him throughout his adult years. (Incidentally, Louis XIII was mildly retarded.)

The taboo against using children sexually is only a few hundred years old. Before then, many infant boys were castrated to enhance their appeal as boy prostitutes. Marriages between boys and adult women were common practice in large European cities until the seventh century. Sex with children was so widespread in Rome "that upper-class boys wore distinctive necklaces lest their fathers engage in sexual behaviour with their own sons by mistake in public bathhouses."[11]

By the seventeenth century sex with children was increasingly called into question. Laws were passed to protect children from adults, and the clergy was warned to become less amorous in its relationships with children. By 1850 not only were adults expected to refrain from this sinful activity but children too were to be kept mindful of the sinfulness of sexuality and especially of masturbation (often called "self-abuse" or "self-pollution"). The "experts" of the time instructed parents to keep candles burning in their children's sleeping quarters; parents could thereby ensure that their children were not masturbating.[12] Servants were warned not to develop close relationships with children, to preclude any sexual developments. And teachers were discouraged from corporal punishment that included beating the child's naked buttocks, since such an activity could produce sexual plea-sure. The movement to regulate children's sinful sexual explo-ration culminated in the 1800s when the medical profession began to recognize children's sexuality and proposed that all pediatric problems could be attributed to early sexual activity. But influential as it was, even this overwhelming concern with children's sexuality did not put a stop to the beating, abandon-ment, or killing of children.[13]

Until well into the early-modern age, infanticide was rou-tine. "Ill-mannered children" — that is, children who cried a lot — or those who were deficient in size or shape, were often killed. The title of one book was *How to Recognize the Newborn That Is Worth Rearing*. If the child fit the accepted norm or seemed worth the expense of energy and food required to raise it, then it stood a fair chance of living beyond its first few months — unless of course it was a girl, for females at the best of times were not highly prized in the family or social hierar-chy, and baby girls were frequently killed. But whether of females or males, of legitimate or illegitimate infants, infanti-cide and the abandonment of infants were common practices.

Philo, a fifth-century Roman soldier and philosopher, speaks of infanticide with candor and an uncommon revul-sion: "Some of them do the deed with their own hands; with monstrous cruelty and barbarity they stifle and throttle the first breath which the infants draw or throw them into a river or into the depths of the sea, after attaching some heavy substance to make them sink more quickly."

A priest from Rome, writing in 1527, complains that "the latrines resound with the cries of children who have been plunged into them."[14] And although the records are scant, when foundling homes opened in England and Europe over two hundred years later, they quickly ran out of room trying to accommodate the great number of abandoned babies. One of the earliest homes was opened by Londoner Thomas Coram, who "couldn't bear to see the dying babies lying in the gutters and rotting on the dung-heaps."[15]

Perhaps the most chilling evidence of the prevalence of infanticide comes from Robert Adamic, who was brought up in an Eastern European village of "killing nurses," a place where mothers knowingly sent their infants to be done away with:

> In her own strange, helpless way, she loved them all . . . but when the luckless infants' parents or the latter's relatives could not or did not pay the customary small sum for their upkeep . . . she disposed of them. . . . One day she returned from the city with an elongated little bundle. . . . A horrible suspicion seized me; the baby in the cradle was going to die! When the baby cried, I heard her get up, and she nursed it in the dark, mumbling, "Poor, poor little one!" I have tried many times since to imagine how she must have felt holding to her breast a child she knew was fated to die by her own hand. . . . "You poor, poor little one!" She purposely spoke clearly so I would be sure to hear. . . . "Fruit of sin through no fault of your own, but sinless in yourself. . . . Soon you will go, soon, my poor one . . . and, going now, you will not go to hell as you would if you lived and grew up and became a sinner." . . . The next morning the child was dead.[16]

If not abandoned, children were almost always sent out to nurse or be cared for in another's home. (This of course depended on social position.) For the adults this was a matter of convenience; for the children the effect could be quite damaging. Until the late sixteenth century, it was thought that if a child were left free it would "scratch its eyes out, tear its ears off, break its legs, distort its bones, be terrified by the sight of its own small limbs, and even crawl about on all fours like an animal."[17] Consequently, whether at home or with a nurse, children were swaddled so tightly and for so long that their circulation could be cut off, and many of them were found with ulcerated skin.

It was also normal for nearly all children to be forced into ice-cold baths every night in order, as the pedàgogues suggested, to build up their fortitude. Beating was simply too common to mention, but the instruments of torture that parents were instructed to use to ensure obedience certainly tell their own story: cats-o'-nine-tails, canes, iron rods, shovels, wooden rods, bundles of sticks, and a whip of small chains called simply "the discipline."

The near-universal revulsion to the sinful condition of the infant, combined with the necessity of breaking its "insolent willfullness," are obvious in this casual letter written by an eighteenth-century American, Esther Burr, to a friend in England. "Oh I almost forgot to tell you, I have begun to govern Sally. She has been whipped on Old Adam's account and she now knows the difference between a smile and a frown as well as I do."[18] Sally was not yet ten months old.

Although I could go on indefinitely about the use and abuse of children during the early-modern period, my intent is not to chronicle the entire history of abuse but to contrast the pre-modern socialization of children with the process as we know it today. This brief and all-too-simplified account of the treatment of children brings us face to face with the possibility of being blinded by our own socialization process. Today we can look back and see that at least some of the practices our ancestors took for granted were unquestionably detrimental to children's physical and emotional development. In most cases I would venture to say that we have learned enough about childhood to enable us to see the brutality inherent in what were common child-rearing practices.

Our own emphathetic response to children is a recent development. Some Western countries continue the brutal child-rearing practices described above. In North America, the message that children have rights — though it is not universally accepted — is more the norm than the exception; there is a genuine movement afoot that recognizes and enhances the world of children and allows them to explore and grow at their own pace. While Western society is not yet so far removed from its past or advanced in its knowledge to comfortably accept evolving concepts of child-rearing, one clear difference between ourselves and our predecessors is that we know now that neither God's representatives nor pedagogues are infallible.

One of the central impulses behind today's concern with child abuse is the knowledge gained over the last decade about the relationship between the events of childhood and later adult development. I believe that the genuine insight into child abuse that spearheaded our concern has now been obscured by panic and the lack of resources to deal with what almost amounts to a reordering of social life. Current legal/psychiatric solutions are misdirected. Alice Miller, a German psychoanalyst and philosopher who writes about child sexual abuse, has provided much-needed insights. Miller writes:

> When we examine the child-rearing literature of the past
> ... we discover the methods that have systematically
> been used to make it impossible for children to realize
> and later to remember the way they were actually treated
> by their parents. Why are the old methods of child-
> raising still so widely employed today? This is a mystery I
> have tried to understand and explain from the perspec-
> tive of the compulsive repetition of the exercise of power.
> Contrary to popular opinion, the injustice, humiliation,
> mistreatment, and coercion a person has experienced
> are not without consequences. The tragedy is that the
> effects of mistreatment are transmitted to new and inno-
> cent victims, even though the victims themselves do not
> remember the mistreatment on a conscious level. . . .
> [They do] not grasp why [they] were being humiliated,
> brushed aside, intimidated, laughed at, treated like an
> object, played with like a doll or brutally beaten.[19]

Miller enjoys a wide and varied readership and is regarded

by her clients and her readers as a modern healer, holding the stature of a Jung or a Freud. Her analysis of German culture carries us into the twentieth century and into contact with some of our more inhumane practices, which were advocated in popular child pedagogy manuals as recently as 1920. Miller attempts to understand the genesis of violence by examining the beliefs and attitudes that make it acceptable to beat, abandon, or brutalize other human beings.

In her books Miller analyzes child-rearing techniques in Germany prior to the Second World War, seeking a link between those early childhood years and Germany's later willingness to accept, consciously, the destruction of European Jewry en masse. This led her to study the Holocaust, a subject that crops up repeatedly among those who study child abuse. Miller concluded that many of the leaders of the Third Reich, including Hitler, were brought up in inordinately disciplined homes and boarding schools where they developed a fear and respect for authority and a rigorous sense of duty. Furthermore, a society that believed that God is dead and assigned His role to whomever could take it by force could eventually elevate the authority of parents, elders, and above all, the state to an equivalent omnipotent status.

The child-rearing techniques used to mould this obedient, dutiful servant of authority were similar to some of the more severe techniques described earlier. The pedagogues suggested brutally beating young children to "drive out willfulness" before it has a chance to become unruly.[20] The manuals recommended step-by-step humiliations to inflict on children to teach them their place in the world. The earlier the better, it was recommended, not only because "the training will take hold faster and more effectively," but also because "the children will not remember later what happened to them." The attitudes of the parents, the schoolmasters, and many of those in charge were, in effect, conspiratorially discharged onto the children from their birth through to their adolescent years, by which time the teachings had taken hold

and the attitudes that society desired were perfectly embod-
ied in them. The litany of horrors that faced them in schools
at the hands of oppressive, punitive teachers completed their
education.

Miller goes on to suggest that the methods used, the humiliations suffered, the autonomy taken away, the beatings — in
fact, nearly all of their childhood experiences — were neatly
stored away in the psyche, waiting to be re-enacted up on their
children or other helpless dependents — in this case, ethnic
minorities and other "displacement objects." In theory, the
love and respect that they were taught and confusedly felt as
children toward their parents collided with the actual rage
and pain that they felt when living those years of abuse. To
avoid the unacceptable or nonsanctioned intense rage
directed toward the parent or the authority, they smothered
all feeling, and it lay dormant for years. It is easy to see how a
generous portion of the population became, as expected,
good, upright citizens — what Rudolf Hess later called
"decent, morally clean," while referring to those upon whom
they vented their unconscious rage as the "Jewish Vermin that
needs to be exterminated for the good of us all."

According to Miller, because of the nearly universal, uniform child pedagogy, Germany's children desired and were
fully capable of following an authority figure who would rule
over an orderly and efficient state. Because feelings of rage
and pain and the capability for self-expression had been cut
off and replaced by obsessive obedience to authority, the
German populace was capable of carrying out the extermina-
tion of Jews and other "deviants." "I was just following
orders," was the single most common line of defence to be
uttered by Nazi war criminals. It was true: through no fault of
their own they had become victims of a child-abuse system, or,
as Miller would say, they were "prisoners of childhood." The
repressed hostility they felt but could not acknowledge was
acted out on the streets of Berlin and in the death camps of
Eastern Europe.

Miller has come to understand the hidden cruelty of restrictive child-rearing practices through the patients in her psychoanalytic practice. She has read extensively the child-rearing manuals that were in common use among turn-of-the-century parents and social leaders. With her penetrating studies of violent criminals, individual leaders of Hitler's Third Reich, and famous artists, Miller may have come very close to explaining the roots of violence, perversity, sadism, and creative genius.

Consider the following passages, written by J. Sulzer in 1748. His teachings became classics in Germany, were read religiously by generations of parents and schoolmasters, and went through numerous printings and updates until the beginning of this century. Sulzer wrote: "If willfulness and wickedness are not driven out, it is impossible to give a child a good education. The moment these flaws appear in a child, it is high time to resist this evil so that it does not become ingrained through habit and the children do not become thoroughly depraved." Willfullness, he says, should be driven out during the first year of life "by means of scolding and the rod. . . . It is always our main purpose to make children into righteous, virtuous persons . . . and to present order to them as something sacred and inviolable."

> [Next comes] obedience to parents and superiors and a trusting acceptance of all they do. . . . It is not very easy, however, to implant obedience in children. . . . One of the advantages of these early years [ages one to three] is that then force and compulsion can be used. Over the years, children forget everything that happened to them in early childhood. If their wills can be broken at this time, they will never remember afterwards that they had a will, and for this very reason the severity that is required will not have any serious consequences.[21]

This type of child-rearing was the norm for generations of German children. And while the pedagogue argues correctly that the children won't remember the severity of the parent's actions, or even be aware that they had a will at one time, it is wrong to think that there will not be serious consequences. (Note the absence of God or religion in these passages; one of the reasons for Sulzer's remarkable success is that he posited a moral framework that was dependent not on God but on human authority figures.)

In the light of present-day psychoanalytic knowledge, children moulded within the confines of such an environment — mental as well as physical — will turn out to be either perfect little automatons with no will of their own (which was the whole point), or severely disturbed adolescents/adults acting out in repetitive, compulsive fashion the trauma of their long-forgotten, repressed childhood experience. And sadly, the reason for their own behavior remains hidden from themselves and from others.

This explains why men can appear for all intents and purposes civilized, while nevertheless existing as soulless, mindless creatures. It explains why the same men who can appreciate classical music, or be moved by flowers blowing in a field, or lavish attention on a pet, can drop bombs that wipe out a city of innocents, for instance, or make corporate decisions to chemically pollute large tracts of land, knowingly endangering thousands of lives.

Miller's work appeared in Germany in 1981 and was translated into English in 1983. Around the same time Miller's book *Thou Shalt Not Be Aware* appeared in Germany, Florence Rush, an American journalist, published her book *The Best-Kept Secret*. Neither woman knew of the other. Both wrote well-documented, revealing accounts of the horrors of childhood. Both books marked a watershed in the histories of child sexual abuse and the evolution of the understanding of childhood.

Florence Rush's discovery of these "horrors," as she called them, came from her historically based research and was strongly supported through her encounters with prostitutes on the streets of major American cities. Eighty per cent of them were drug addicts and most were involved in exceedingly brutal relationships with their pimps. As Rush gained their confidence she learned that nearly seventy per cent of them had been sexually abused as children. Her published results of course strengthened the position of child advocates. Alice Miller had also noted that a number of her patients had been sexually abused and had repressed the experience, only to later find themselves acting in ways that repeated the original trauma without revealing it — Freud's repetition compulsion.

It is interesting that Miller's accounts of child sexual abuse came reluctantly out of the depths of her patients' unconscious during her analytic sessions. There she saw the wounded child stumbling painfully into adulthood and found that healing came through an empathetic analysis that allowed the patient to regress to the source of the original trauma, a process not unlike Janov's "primal scream" therapy. Acknowledging sexual abuse as a real trauma — rather than considering it mere sexual fantasy as most Freudians do — Miller claims that she was able to achieve a high level of healing among her patients. Rush, on the other hand, confirmed the discovery she had first made in historical archives by talking to hookers on the streets of Manhattan and San Francisco, who loudly proclaimed the effects of their childhood traumas. Rush believed that until women like herself had come along, few had bothered to listen to these women's stories.

Another important study came at this time, once again from a psychiatrist's casebook. Bennet Braun of Chicago, director of the Dissociative Disorder Program at Rush-Presbyterian–St. Luke Medical Center at Rush University, became fascinated with the underlying psychic mechanism that resulted in multiple personalities. There are two recurring themes for sufferers of this disorder: uncontrolled dissociation, and a childhood history of severe and repeated abuse by parents and other family members. Women are more likely to suffer from multiple-personality disorders than are men because, say the researchers, women are more often the victims of sexual abuse. By unconsciously dissociating themselves from the various traumas that they must face, these women experience what has come to be known as a multiple personality. As they dissociate, new personalities form, which take on different tasks in their day-to-day lives. One of the most popular and rivetting accounts of multiple-personality disorder is the book *Sybil* by Flora Schreiber, which explored a multi-faceted consciousness with different needs, wants, desires, and memories clustered around a series of personalities, some of which knew the others existed, and some of which didn't. Sybil's story made it clear that severe abuse in childhood is at the root of this disorder, although at the time this revelation was lost amidst the novelty of the disorder itself and Sybil's efforts to come to terms with it. The public simply wasn't receptive to this kind of scientific information. But Braun and other psychiatrists studying the disorder generated popular support, while his own shocking revelations provided further scientific backing to the claims of Miller and her successors.

Braun studied 126 case histories of multiple-personality disorders from 126 independent psychiatrists. He had called for the papers on a random basis, asking only for classic symptomology. Ninety to ninety-five per cent of these cases involved gross sexual abuse during childhood. This was not news to Braun or others in his field. Indeed it was something he expected when scanning for classic symptomology.

What was startling, however, was that twenty per cent of the cases "reported some form of satanic involvement." At a later conference, Braun asked the attending doctors to document any cases of satanic ritual that they had encountered among their patients. When the cases poured in from all over the country, the rate jumped to thirty-two per cent.

Braun states that he is uncertain what to make of this claim, that the scientist in him needs more proof. However, he goes on to say that the same story is told by numerous patients from different parts of the country with a consistency that, "if untrue, would be even more astonishing. What does that tell us about the mind or the unconscious?" He is not as willing to dismiss these stories as he was when he first began hearing them. What puzzles him about these confessions is that they come out under hypnosis, at a time when the patients have no idea what they are saying and no reason to invent such incriminating information. Braun has never found any physical evidence of satanic rituals among his own patients, even though he had treated more than fifty persons who claim to have been involved in satanic rituals.

What is one to make of Braun's study? As he himself asks, if the tales are not true, what do they tell us about the mind, about the dark myths we carry within us? That such tales might be true is not, in my opinion, credible.

In this chapter we have made another long excursion into history in an attmept to shed light on the phenomenon of child sexual abuse. We are gradually being made aware that gross abuse in childhood leads to a variety of psychological afflictions, some with criminal implications. What does that tell us about our mores? What does that tell us about sadism, sexuality, and satanism, the cornerstones of the children's allegations in the trials with which this book began? What does it tell us about men?

It should tell us at one level that child abuse is as multifaceted as the mind. And the deeper we go into a mind that is painfully at odds with itself, the more we discover what William Gaylin believes exists in all of us — incestuous, cannibalistic, murderous urges, fantasies so dark that, if we must bring them out, we clothe them in satanic majesty. There must be a reason for so frequently encountering this dark side of the unconscious in madmen, in women, and in children. We may already have answered our questions, to some degree, in the case of children. They are being led to consider this set of images by workers who are predisposed to believe it or who trigger this fantasy in them through traumatic investigation into the children's lives.

These studies also tell us something about males. If we look to the priests and judges of the Inquisition, who mainly tortured women (male victims were nearly always politically chosen), or to the fathers who placed their naked sons in cellars and whipped them "for their own good," or to the fathers who beat their wives in front of the children like Albert DeSalvo, or at the man DeSalvo later becomes who hunts down and rapes or murders women — if we look at all this, men are the enemy. But if we look at the cumulative image that emerges from the history of childhood, we see that, more accurately, these men act in cycles: victim-victimizer-victim, through the generations. We are all victims to some degree.

Since the publications of Braun's and Miller's works in North America hundreds of articles in mainstream national and local media have given voice to this concern with childhood. Over thirty books on child abuse have since been written, most of them supporting the information that Rush and Miller articulated, but in highly personal, emotionally charged, confessional styles. In 1987, seven books were published in the United States alone dealing with the problems of children, the law, and false accusations.

And here we return to the social phenomenon that initiated the study for this book. In the wake of the tidal wave of outraged public interest that followed the publication of these works, offenders were vigorously stalked and their child victims saved from what many were convinced was and would continue to be a living nightmare. But while the message of psychohistorians and journalists like Rush and Miller formed the intellectural underpinnings of this rapidly growing movement, the social realities of child abuse became mired in the increasingly emotional and complex atmosphere of child-abuse regulatory procedures. How does one get to the roots of violence? How does one get inside families and make crucial decisions affecting their lives, and on what pretext? The mistake that North American child-care workers made is that long before settling the extremely tangled psychological and legal questions that must be answered, they have activated a premature legalistic response as the solution in all cases.

The facts of child abuse do indeed justify our intense concern with this issue. But can we adequately rush into an area that has taken centuries merely to acknowledge? Shouldn't we precede our actions with a period of sober, serious reflection? The facts, figures, and fears that are now making the rounds and stirring up a hysterical climate are replete with emotional biases, misinformed zealots, over-worked prescriptions, untenable premises, poorly planned objectives, and divisive strategies. We need more healers.

Until then, we are doing a disservice to the children we are purporting to save and to the parents we believe we are saving them from.

EPILOGUE

It may be worthwhile to end this analysis with a comment on Sigmund Freud. Ironically, at a time in Western history when sex and death and childhood are openly and intensely discussed, the founder of psychoanalysis has fallen into disrepute. Few today take Freud's drive theory seriously, at least not without serious reservations and qualifications.

It was Freud after all who bequeathed to us a notion of infantile sexuality and opened up to exploration the uncharted area of the mind. It was Freud who gave to us a notion of man as a sensually driven beast, capable of killing his father, marrying his mother, and eating the flesh to hide the crime. Freud had looked into the deep pit of the mind and reeled back into the safety of speculation.

In 1896, the year before he published the completely altered and monumentally influential *Origins of Psychoanalysis*, Freud gave a lecture entitled "The Aetiology of Hysteria." His pioneering discovery was predicated on what to him were unequivocal findings. Freud reported that of eighteen cases of hysterical illness treated by him (six men and twelve women), all the patients had been sexually abused by an adult or an older sibling, who had in turn also been abused by an adult. None of the eighteen patients were aware of this fact when they began their treatment. If they had been conscious of it, he said, there would have been no symptoms and no need for psychoanalytic treatment. This astonishing revelation proved totally unacceptable to the Victorians' prudish respectability; it has since been relegated to the archives of psychoanalysis.

Freud taught us that these childhood traumas resulted in crippling neuroses; though not consciously recalled, the traumas are manifested in destructive and self-destructive behavior and crippling delusions and dreams. But in 1897, just one year later, Freud abandoned this theory altogether. He stated instead that the infantile sexual scenes recalled in analysis were far too prevalent to be true (which was precisely why he had accepted them in the first place) and replaced his hard-won explorer's knowldge with drive theory, at the heart of which is the notion of infantile sexual fantasy. Freud and his orthodox followers now treated everything the adult patient told them about physical or sexual abuse in childhood as a manifestation of innate aggressive or sexual instincts.

Freud went on to write about civilization and its discontents. He told us much about successfully psychoanalyzed patients who, through analysis, escaped from their various neuroses. Such people would not necessarily be happy, but they would be rid of their delusions and would therefore stand a far better chance of living honestly and sanely in the world.

But if his critics are right — and the evidence is clearly set out by Freud himself — he himself suffered a delusion for the better part of his adult years and passed that delusion on to the many psychoanalysts and psychiatrists who followed him. Even Freud, say his critics, had not awakened from the nightmare that constitutes childhood for a large portion of the Western world's population.

As Gail Rubin suggests in her book *Pleasure and Danger*, in a passage that neatly sums up the message of the present book and the essential difficulties within the complex of child-abuse issues:

> The time has come to think about sex. Contemporary conflicts over sexual values and erotic conduct have much in common with the religious disputes of earlier centuries. They acquire immense symbolic value and

centuries. They acquire immense symbolic value and become the vehicle for displacing other social anxieties. To some people, sexuality may seem an unimportant topic or a frivolous diversion from the more critical problems of poverty, war, disease, racism, famine, or nuclear annihilation. But it's precisely at times such as these, when we live with the possibility of unthinkable destruction, that people are liable to become danger-ously crazy about sexuality. Each sex scare or morality campaign deposits new regulations as a kind of fossil record of its passage.[1]

We must now think about sex. We must think about AIDS, which links sex and death. Somehow sex and death and vio-lence come together in our world in a way that wasn't true even a generation ago. We must now think about men whose sole drive is to stalk and sadistically rape and murder inno-cent women and children. We must think about the stories of horrid sexual abuse being told by an unprecedented number of children.

Yes, the time has come to think — and to talk — about sex.

But must we speak with our children about it? When chil-dren speak to us about sexuality and death, mirroring our world back to us — such as it is — we are justified in equating the two. Children appear to be bearing the brunt of the bur-den we have created. They have been taught to fear for their personal safety. They have been taught that they live in a world without purpose. Science tells them that they live on a planet in the middle of a galactic highway that stretches on for milky-ways of unknowable cosmic distance, and that from this universe God is absent. They have no certainty that they will have a future. This is the world they have inherited.

North American children watch on average four hours of television a day. It is difficult to assess how they view the world when they are inundated with TV's strangled visual/verbal images. Marshall McLuhan taught us that these images would have a far greater impact on the new generation of children than on any previous generation. Neil Postman goes so far as to say that television blurs the distinctions between childhood aspirations and adult secrets, that television offers broadly based knowledge about sex and death and failure and does so in the crassest commerical context, without the children having undergone any rite of passage that might help give them a perspective on the knowledge they are gaining. In a sense, they are being deprived of the childhood innocence we as a society have come to value and try to protect. We don't know what living in such troubled times does to children, and all of us want it to be better for them.

Health-care professionals believe that they have uncovered the roots of violence. They believe that children don't lie about abuse, and they have brought the sullied victims of child abuse off the street and out to center stage to give dramatic performances before professional, public, and government audiences alike. They speak of more than a million children being mercilessly beaten with cords, shovels, belts, and frying pans. They tell us heart-rending tales of discipline wherein wayward children — for the slightest offences — are forced to place their hands on the hot elements of electric stoves, face confinement in damp basements with scarely any food, and other barbaric practices that we thought were driven out of civilization along with flogging and public hangings. And even while this image of emaciated, beaten children sinks uneasily into our collective consciousness, we are asked to acknowledge once and for all that child sexual abuse is a rampant social disease that knows no boundaries. It exists on the streets in the form of sadomasochistic relationships between pimps and prostitutes; it exists in one out of every four North American households in the form of incestuous relationships; it is perpetrated for the most part against powerless young females.

Today's child advocates are profoundly moved by the plight of our children. They are attempting to do their best, with their limited resources, to rid the world of the scourge that is child abuse. But the result, despite their best intentions, is to commit injustice of a magnitude that is difficult to comprehend in a free and democratic society. In seeking to identify and treat the greatest number of abused children, social agencies have lobbied successfully for broader reporting laws. In the U.S., which first charted the course that Canadians are now following, it is estimated that more than 500,000 families each year are investigated for allegations that turn out to be unfounded.

Child advocates have succeeded beyond their wildest dreams in changing societal values where the issue of child abuse is concerned. They have convinced the government and the public that the child-abuse problem is so widespread, the offenders so diverse in their characteristics, and the consequences so ghastly that special interventionary measures are needed to deal with it. These measures include "enter and apprehend" and closed-door decision-making processes that permanently affect the lives of families. Neither parents nor children who undergo such investigations are ever quite the same afterward.

In his summation to the Hamilton trial, Judge Beckett observed that the decision he was required to make about removing the children from their home into the arms of the state was one of the most profound decisions a judge could make. He based it on two years worth of evidence. The officials of the Hamilton–Wentworth Children's Aid Society had taken only two interviews to reach their decision. At the conclusion of the trial, despite the mother's tragic history and the law enforcement agencies' reluctance to attempt prosecution, the CAS tried to revive the matter within the criminal justice system. Because of lack of evidence, the police concluded that they did not have a case. But what purpose would laying criminal charges have served? Would it have helped the mother? Would it have helped the children? Would it have helped the public?

As the public becomes aware that unfounded reports are

falsely inflating abuse statistics, they will respond less favorably to truly abused children. And it is these children, these beaten and abused children, who need the best of our resources and directed compassion. Unless changes are made now, the potentially valuable force of public concern will serve only to increase mistrust and hysteria. We must direct our ablest medical and legal professionals, psychologists, and community workers to look again at the problems and to propose more humane and more effective solutions.

END NOTES

Chapter 1. The Hamilton Trial
1. The material for Chapter 1 was taken from court transcripts, submissions from all of the lawyers, Judge Thomas Beckett's final summation, newspaper articles, court notes, and interviews. The director of the Hamilton-Wentworth Children's Aid Society and the Society's legal representative declined to speak with the author about the case during the course of the original trial or during the appeal process.

Chapter 2. A Legal Dilemma
1. Coleman, Lee, "False Allegations of Child Sexual Abuse: Have the Experts Been Caught with their Pants Down?" 1985, pp. 26–7, unpublished.
2. Underwager, Ralph, Personal communication with author, August 1987.
3. Hugh Stanton, Jr., District Attorney General, Memphis, Tennessee, in communication with Ken Lanning, Special Agent, FBI, concerning Memphis child-care case. Flight is a common element in many children's stories in these kinds of cases.
4. From a series of articles which appeared in the Sacramento *Bee* from 27 October to 19 August 1985.
5. Hollida Wakefield and Ralph Underwager, *Accusations of Child Sexual Abuse* (Springfield, IL: Charles C. Thomas, 1987), p. 71.
6. Hubert H. Humphrey III, *Report on Scott County Investigation*, Feb. 12, 1985.
7. The following section was culled from the reports of the trial in the *New York Times*, from Jan Hollingsworth's book *Unspeakable Acts* (1986), and from the author's personal communication with Drs. Underwager and Summit (1987), both of whom attended the trial, and from a later related symposium in Canada.
8. Wakefield and Underwager, pp. 39, 87.

Chapter 3. The North American Experience
1. Barbara Nelson, *Making an Issue of Child Abuse: Political Agenda-Setting for Social Problems* (Chicago: University of Chicago Press, 1984), p. 6.
2. Ibid., p. 13.
3. C. Henry Kempe and F.N. Silverman, "The Battered Child Syndrome," *Journal of the American Medical Association* 181 (1962), 17–24.
4. National Center on Child Abuse and Neglect, *Executive Summary: National Study of the Incidence and Severity of Child Abuse*, DHHS Publica-

tion No. 81–30325 (Washington, DC: Government Printing Office, 1981).

5. Besharov, 1985, p. 25.
6. Ibid., p. 26.
7. Ibid., p. 26.
8. Ibid., p. 27; Underwager, p. 99.
9. Besharov, p. 28.
10. Ibid., 1985, pp. 25 and 28.
11. Ibid., p. 21.
12. Levitt, ed., *Royal Commission on Family and Children's Law* (Berger Commission), 1984, p. 13.
13. Ibid., p. 93.
14. *Badgeley Report*, p. 1061.
15. Ibid., Vol. I.
16. Ibid., p. 1073.
17. Sgroi, Suzanne, Perspectives in Child Sexual Abuse, Conference in Toronto, July 1987, tapes 1–5.
18. Wakefield and Underwager, op. cit., pp. 401–478.
19. Sgroi, Toronto Conference, tape 3, "Child Victims of Sexual Abuse".
20. Sgroi, Suzanne, *Handbook of Clinical Intervention in Child Sexual Abuse*, 1982, pp. 58–9.
21. Coleman, op. cit., p. 27.

Chapter 4. Satanism
1. Hamilton *Spectator*, 30 March 1987.
2. Ibid.
3. Dr. Otto Weininger interview with Frank Jones, October 1986, Toronto *Star* columnist.
4. Jeffry Burton Russell, *A History of Witchcraft: Sorcerers, Heretics, and Pagans* (London: Thames and Hudson, 1982), pp. 111–131.
5. E. Burman, *Inquisition: The Hammer of Heresy* (N.p.: The Aquarian Press, 1984), p. 181.
6. Ibid., p. 131.
7. B. Hamilton, *Medieval Inquisition: Foundations of Medieval History* (New York: Holmes and Meier, 1981), p. 93.
8. Joseph Klaits, *Servants of Satan: The Age of the Witch-Hunts* (Bloomington: Indiana University Press, 1985), p. 107.
9. Sir A.G. Cardew, *A Short History of the Inquisition* (London: Watts and Co., 1933), p. 61.
10. Klaits, p. 157.
11. Hamilton, p. 119.
12. Russell, p. 267.
13. Stephen Nissenbaum and Paul Boyer, "A Clash of Two Worlds," in *Witches and Historians*, ed. Marc Mappen (Melbourne, FL: Robert E. Krieger Publishing, 1980), pp. 32–39.
14. Klaits, p. 155.

Chapter 5. Sadism
1. K. Freund, G. Heasman, and V. Roper, "Results of the Main Studies on Sexual Offences against Children and Pubescents," *Canadian Journal of Criminology* 24 (1982): 17–21.
2. Burgess, op. cit., pp. 89–101.
3. Wakefield and Underwager, op. cit., p. 287, forthcoming.
4. Ibid., pp. 281–293.
5. FBI Subcommittee on Government Information, Justice, and Agriculture, United States House of Representatives, April, 1986.
6. Reno Gazette Journal, March 22, 1984.
7. Elliot Leyton, *Hunting Humans: The Rise of the Modern Mass Murderer* (Toronto: McClelland & Stewart, 1986), p. 86.
8. Rae George, *Confessions of the Boston Strangler*, p. 27.

Chapter 6. The Roots of Violence
1. Despert quoted in Lloyd Demause, "The Evolution of Childhood", in Lloyd Demause, ed., *The History of Childhood* (New York: Psychohistory Press) p. 6.
2. L. Shultz, "Child Sexual Abuse in Historical Perspective," *Journal of Human Sexuality and Social Work* 1 (1982), p. 11.
3. Demause in Demause, p. 8.
4. Ibid., p. 49.
5. Joseph Illick, in "Child-rearing Practices in Seventeenth Century England and America", Demause, p. 316.
6. Christophe Meckel, *Wanted: My Father's Portrait*, trans. by author (Dusseldorf: Claasson, 1980), p. 89.
7. Ibid.
8. Quoted in Illick, p. 329.
9. Demause, op. cit. p. 14.
10. Ibid.
11. Shultz, p. 21.
12. Philippe Ariès, *Centuries of Childhood: A Social History of Family Life*, trans. Robert Baldrick (New York: Vintage, 1962), p. 89.
13. Ibid., pp. 71–87.
14. Demause, p. 39.
15. Ibid., p. 29.
16. Ibid., p. 30.
17. Ibid., p. 32.
18. Illick, p. 321.
19. Alice Miller, *Prisoners of Childhood* [published in paperback as *The Drama of the Gifted Child* (1983)] (New York: Basic Books, 1983), p. 247.
20. Ibid., p. 11.
21. Ibid., p. 12–13.

Epilogue.
1. Rubin, Gail. "Ideas" script for CBC, Sept. 1987.

BIBLIOGRAPHY

Child Abuse/Child Welfare and Development

Ariès, Philippe. *Centuries of Childhood: A Social History of Family Life*. (Trans. by Robert Baldrick) New York: Vintage, 1962.

Cohen, M.L., T. Seghorn, and W. Calnas, "Sociometric Study of the Sex Offender." *Journal of Abnormal Psychology* 74 (1969): 249–55.

Davidson, H.A. "Sexual Exploitation of Children: An Overview of its Scope, Impact, and Legal Ramifications." *FBI Law Enforcement Bulletin* No. 2, 1984.

Finkelhor, David. *Sexually Victimized Children*. New York: Free Press, 1979.

————. *Child Sexual Abuse: New Theory and Research*. New York: Free Press, 1984.

————. "Sexual Abuse in the National Incidence Study of Child Abuse and Neglect: An Appraisal." *Child Abuse and Neglect* 8 (1984): 23–32.

Freund, K., G. Heasman, and V. Roper. "Results of the Main Studies on Sexual Offences against Children and Pubescents." *Canadian Journal of Criminology* 24 (1982): 387–97.

Groth, A.N. "Sexual Trauma in the Life Histories of Rapists and Child Molesters." *Victimology* 4 (1979): 10–16.

Kempe, C. Henry, and F.N. Silverman. "The Battered Child Syndrome." *Journal of the American Medical Association* 181 (1962): 17–24.

————. *The Common Secret: Sexual Abuse of Children and Adolescents*. New York: Freeman, 1984.

Mause, Lloyd de, ed. *The History of Childhood*. New York: Psychohistory Press, 1974.

Meckel, Christoph. *Wanted: My Father's Portrait*. (Trans. by author) Dusseldorf: Claassen, 1980.

Miller, Alice. *Prisoners of Childhood* (published in paperback as *The Drama of the Gifted Child* [1983]). New York: Basic books, 1981.

————. *For Your Own Good: Hidden Cruelty in Child-Rearing and the Roots of Violence*. (Trans. by Hildegarde and Hunter Hannum) New York: Farrar, Straus, Giroux, 1983.

————. *Thou Shalt Not Be Aware: Psychoanalysis and Society's Betrayal of the Child*. (Trans. by Hildegarde and Hunter Hannam) New York: Farrar, Straus, Giroux, 1984.

National Center on Child Abuse and Neglect. *Executive Summary: National Study of the Incidence and Severity of Child Abuse and Neglect* (DHHS Publication No. 81-30325). Washington, D.C.: U.S. Government Printing Office, 1981.

Nelson, Barbara. *Making an Issue of Child Abuse: Political Agenda-Setting for Social Problems*. Chicago: University of Chicago Press, 1984.

Pearce, Joseph Chilton. *Magical Child: Rediscovering Nature's Plan for Our Children*. New York: Bantam, 1977.

Postman, Neil. *The Disappearance of Childhood*. New York: Delacorte, 1982.

Rush, Florence. *The Best-Kept Secret: Sexual Abuse of Children*. Englewood Cliffs, N.J.: Prentice-Hall, 1980.

Shultz, L. "Child Sexual Abuse in Historical Perspective." *Journal of Human Sexuality and Social Work* 1 (1982): 21-35.

Sgroi, Suzanne M. *Handbook of Clinical Intervention in Child Sexual Abuse*. Toronto: D.C. Heath, 1982.

Summit, R. "The Child Sexual Abuse Accommodation Syndrome." *Child Abuse and Neglect* 7 (1983): 177-93.

Wakefield, Hollida, and Ralph Underwager. *Accusations of Child Sexual Abuse*. Springfield, IL: Charles C. Thomas, forthcoming.

Sex/Satanism/The Inquisition

Anglo, Sydney. *The Damned Art: Essays in the Literature of Witchcraft*. London: Routledge & Kegan Paul, 1977.

Bullough, Vern L. *Sexual Variance in Society and History*. Chicago: University of Chicago Press, 1980.

Burman, E. *Inquisition: The Hammer of Heresy*. N.p.: The Aquarian Press, 1984.

Cardew, Sir A.G. *A Short History of the Inquisition*. London: Watts and Co., 1933.

Gilson, Etienne. *Reason and Revelation in the Middle Ages*. New York: Scribner's, 1938.

Hamilton, Bernard. *Medieval Inquisition: Foundations of Medieval History*. New York: Holmes and Meier, 1981.

Hemphill, R.E. "Historical Witchcraft and Psychiatric Illness in Western Europe." *Proceedings of the Royal Society of Medicine* LIX, 1966.

Kelly, Henry A. *Towards the Death of Satan: The Growth and Decline of Christian Demonology*. London: Chapman, 1968.

King, Francis. *Sexuality, Magic, and Perversion*. Secaucus, NJ: Citadel Press, 1972.

Klaits, Joseph. *Servants of Satan: The Age of the Witch-Hunts*. Bloomington: Indiana University Press, 1985.

LaVey, Anton S. *Satanic Bible*. London: W.H. Allen, 1977.

———. *The Satanic Rituals*. New York: Avon, 1972.

Mappen, Marc, ed. *Witches and Historians: Interpretations of Salem*. Melbourne, FL: Robert E. Krieger Publishing, 1980.

Martello, Leo. *Black Magic, Satanism, and Voodoo*. N.p.: HC Publishers, 1973.

Murray, Margaret. "Child Sacrifice Among European Witches." *Man*, 1918.

———. *The Witch-Cult in Western Europe*. Oxford: Clarendon Press, 1921.

Nissenbaum, Stephen, and Paul Boyer. "A Clash of Two Worlds." *Witches and Historians*, ed. Marc Mappen. Melbourne, FL: Robert E. Krieger Publishing, 1980.

Russell, Jeffry Burton. *A History of Witchcraft: Sorcerers, Heretics, and Pagans*. London: Thames and Hudson, 1981.

————. *Witchcraft in the Middle Ages*. Ithaca, NY: Cornell University Press, 1972.

Spence, Lewis. *Encyclopaedia of Occultism*. (Originally published by Routledge & Sons, London, 1920.) New York: University Books, 1960.

Zacharias, Gerhard. *The Satanic Cult*. (Trans. by Christine Trollope) London: Allen and Unwin, 1964.

Violent Crimes/Criminals

Banks, Harold. *The Strangler! The Story of the Terror in Boston*. New York: Avon, 1967.

Bugliosi, Vincent, and Curt Gentry. *Helter Skelter: The True Story of the Manson Murders*. New York: Bantam, 1975.

Frank, Gerold. *The Boston Strangler*. New York: New American Library, 1967.

Leyton, Elliot. *Hunting Humans: The Rise of the Modern Mass Murderer*. Toronto: McClelland & Stewart, 1986.

Lunde, Donald. *Murder and Madness*. San Francisco: San Francisco Book Company, 1976.

Macdonald, John. *The Murderer and His Victim*. Springfield, IL: Thomas, 1961.

"Violent Crime." *FBI Law Enforcement Bulletin* No. 54, 1985.

Wilson, Colin. *A Casebook of Murder*. New York: Cowles Book Co., 1970.

————, and Donald Seaman. *Encyclopaedia of Modern Murder*. New York: Putnam, 1985.

Winn, Steven, and David Merril. *Ted Bundy: The Killer Next Door*. New York: Bantam, 1980.

INDEX

Abbott, Jack Henry, 141
Abuse, definitions of, 72
Abuse hotline, 77, 100
Abuse register, 98
Accommodation syndrome theory. *See*
 Summit, Dr. Roland
Adamic, Robert, 166
Adoption Act (Canada), 82
"Aetiology of Hysteria, The" (Sigmund
 Freud), 178
American Society for the Prevention of
 Cruelty to Animals (ASPCA), 66
Anatomically correct dolls, 19, 49, 103–
 04
Ariès, Philippe, 156
Aristotle, 113
Atkins, Susan, 150
Attitudes towards children, 64–66

Baca, Hon. Robert T., 97
Badgley Report, 83–88, 89, 90
Basque witch trials (1610), 123
"Battered Child Syndrome, The", 68–
 69, 73
Beckett, Judge Thomas, 1, 5–6, 15, 25,
 28, 56, 130, 135, 182
Bell, Doris, 37–41, 51, 111
Bentzes, 42, 44–46, 50–51
Berger Commission, 79–81
Berger, Hon. Thomas R., 79–80
Bergh, Henry, 66
Besherov, Douglas, 78
Best-Kept Secret, The (Florence Rush),
 172–73
Bill C–15 (Ontario), 22, 88–90, 91
Black Death, 115
Blake, Danny (see footnote, p. 1), 3–4,
 6, 8, 14–15, 22, 23–24
Bonnie and Clyde, 140
Boston Strangler, the, 152–53
Bowen, Sergeant David, 16
Boyer, Paul, 126
Brady, Ian (Moors Murders), xiii, 137,
 138, 141–43
Braga, Joseph, 57–60
Braga, Laurie, 57–58

Braun, Bennet, 173
Brooks (Corll case), 146–47
Brown, Helen, 43–44
Brown, Tom, 30, 43–44
Buchan, Cindy, 47, 48, 51
Buchan, Don, 47, 48, 51
Bundy, Ted, xiii, 140, 144–46, 152
Burgess pedophile study, 131–32
Burn out, of child abuse investigators,
 76–77
Burr, Anna, 156
Burr, Esther, 167

Caldwell, George, 91
Canadian Association of Criminal
 Defense Lawyers, 88
Cannibalism, 11, 39, 109
Capone, Al, 140
Case, Francis, 66
Case, Mary Ellen, 66
Catholic Children's Aid Society, 105
Centre for the Prevention of Child
 Abuse (Ontario), 100
Ceremonies, pagan, 112–13
Chamberlain, Dr., 130
Child Abuse/Neglect Policy Handbook, 100,
 101
Child Abuse Prevention and
 Treatment Act (U.S., 1974), 69
Child Abuse Registry, 100, 105
Childhood experiences and later adult
 development, 7–8, 152–53, 155–57,
 168–76
Child molesters. *See* Pedophiles
Child murderers, 130–31, 136
Child Paternity Act (Canada), 82
Child-rearing techniques, in history,
 158–68, 169–71
Children's Aid Society (CAS), 29, 65, 95
 See also Hamilton–Wentworth
 Children's Aid Society; Ontario
 Association of Children's Aid
 Societies.
"Child Sexual Abuse Accommodation
 Syndrome, The " (Roland Summit),
 18, 96

Cleaver, Robert, 161
Commission on Child Welfare in
    Canada. *See* Berger Commission
Communication of abuse stories, 127–
    28
Community trauma, 55
Connolly, Mary, 66
Coram, Thomas, 165
Corll, Dean Allen, 146–47
Corroborating evidence, 35–36, 54–55,
    60, 88, 91, 109, 112
Cross-germination of witnesses, 54
Cult Awareness Network (U.S.), 109
Cult Project (Montreal), 109

Daddy's Girl, 71
Dade County case, 57–60, 112
Dark Ages, 113–14
Daycare centers, 92
Daycare programs, 82
de Mause, Lloyd, 155, 157, 160
Department of Social Services (New
    York State), 73–74
de Rais, Gilles, 140, 142
de Sade, Marquis, 142
DeSalvo, Albert (the Boston Strangler),
    137, 152–53, 176
Despert, J. Louise, 156
Dill, Claudia, 37
Dill, Gary, 36–37, 38
Dionysus, 112–13
Dissociative Disorder Program (Rush
    University), 173
Dominican Order, 114
Donnelly, Tricia, 9
Dougherty, District Attorney John, 37
"Drive" theory, 178, 179
Dworkin, Andrea, 71

Elizabeth (Hamilton case) (see
    footnote, p. 1), 10
Elliot Lake case, 105–06
*Emotionally Disturbed Child, Then and
    Now, The* (Despert, J. Louise), 156
Evidence, corroborating. *See*
    Corroborating evidence
Exclusion of accused from courtroom
    during child's testimony, 88

Family and Child Services Act
    (Canada), 82, 105
Family Relations Act (Canada), 82
Farraway, David, 148
Fassel, Mary Lou, 89
Federal Bureau of Investigation (FBI),

x, 52, 133–34, 136
Feminists, 70–71, 88–90, 134–35
Ferrin, Darlene, 149
Finkelhor, David, 132
For Your Own Good (Alice Miller), 155
Foundling homes, 165
Freud, Sigmund, 61, 108, 110, 157, 173,
    178–79
Freund pedophile study, 131
Fuster, Frank, 58, 60, 112
Fuster, Iliana, 58, 60

Gareau, Maurice, 104–05
Gaylin, William, 139, 175
Gede, Dr. Eva, 5, 23, 24–25
Giaretto, Henry, 94–95
Godly Form of Household, A, 161
Goldman, Scotty, 57
Good, Sarah, 124–25
"Good touch/bad touch" programs, 92,
    93, 96
Gordon, Corey L., 93
Grimes study on sexual abuse, 132

Hamilton case, vii, 1–29, 182
Hamilton–Wentworth Children's Aid
    Society 1, 2, 8, 15–16, 18–22, 182. *See
    also* Children's Aid Society; Ontario
    Association of Children's Aid
    Societies
Hammer of Witches, The (*Malleus
    Maleficarum*), 116
Harold, Margaret, 147
Harper, John, 17
Hartrick, Michael, 13
Hausmannin, Walpurga, 120–21
Heasman pedophile study, 131
Henley, Wayne, 146–47
Heroard, 163–64
"Hero" serial murderers, 139
Hess, Rudolf, 170
Hindley, Myra (Moors Murders), 137,
    141–43
History of Childhood, The (Lloyd de
    Mause), 160
Hitler, Adolf, 169
Holman, John Paul, 36–37
*How to Recognize the Newborn That Is
    Worth Rearing*, 165
Humphrey, Hubert H., III, x, 1, 53–54

Id, the, 110
In the Belly of the Beast (Jack Henry
    Abbott), 141
Infanticide, 165–66

Inquisition, the, 114–22, 129
Interrogation/interviews, 54–55, 102–04, 111, 118–22, 126–29
Investigation of abuse, 16, 21–22, 41, 49, 52, 77, 100–04

Janov, 173
Jensen, Betty Lou, 148
Jordan case, ix–x, 1, 42–55, 125, 127
Journal of the American Medical Association, 68
Jung, C.G., 108

Kempe, C. Henry, 68–69
Kiss Daddy Goodnight, 71
Knight, William (see footnote, p. 1), 2, 5, 8–10, 15, 19–20, 22, 24–25
Kronos (Greek god), 112

Langevin, Dr., 24
Langevin study on sexual abuse, 132
Lang study on sexual abuse, 132
LeBar, Father Frank, viii, 108–09, 111
Le Dranque, Pierre, 123
Lee, John Alvin, 64
Levitt, K.L., 80
Lewkowitz, Rick, 36, 37
Louis XIII, 163–64

MacCauley Institute, 40, 41
Macleod, Charles, 109
McLuhan, Marshall, 180
McMartin, Virginia, 41–42
Mageau, Michael, 149
Mailer, Norman, 141
Malleus Maleficarum. See Hammer of Witches, The
Manhattan Beach (California) case, x, xi, 41–42
Manson, Charles, xi, 56, 137, 150–51, 152
Mather, Cotton, 124, 161–62
Mead, Dr. John, 110
Meckel, Christoph, 161
Media/murderer relationship, 150
Mental Health Legislation Act (Canada), 82
Metropolitan Toronto Special Committee on Child Abuse, 92
Miller, Alice, 79, 155, 157, 168–71, 172, 173
Ministry of Community and Social Services (Ontario), 100
Ministry of Human Resources (Ontario), 100

Minnesota case, 75–76
Minnesota Multiphasic Personality Inventory (MMPI), 130–31, 132, 133
Moors Murderers, xiii, 137, 138, 141–43
Morris, Kathleen, ix–x, 47–51, 127
Multiple personalities, 4, 5, 107, 173–75
Murder, 10–11, 39, 51–53
Murderers, child, 130–31, 136
Mutilation, 11, 39, 51–53
Myers, George, 47
Myers, Jane, 47

Nasmith, Judge Peter, 63, 106
National Center for Child Abuse and Neglect (U.S.), 69–70, 71, 74, 78, 83
Naysmith, Bette, 109
Ng, Charles, xiii, 140
Nissenbaum, Stephen, 126

Olson, Clifford, xiii, 140
"On Establishing Trust with Incest Victims" (Doris Bell), 39
Ontario Association of Children's Aid Societies, 91
Ontario Institute for Studies in Education (OISE), 110
Origins of Psychoanalysis (Sigmund Freud), 178
Osborne, Sarah, 124–25

Pagan ceremonies, 112–13
Parris, Reverend Samuel, 124
Pediatricians, 68–69
Pedophilia, 19–20, 130–32, 135–36, 156, 164–65
Philo, 165
Pleasure and Danger (Gail Rubin), 179–80
Polymorphous perverse pleasure, 61
Pornographic literature, 9–10, 139
Pornography: Men Possessing Women (Andrea Dworkin), 71
Possession by the devil, 123–25
Postman, Neil, 180–81
Potter, Beverly Anne (see footnote, p. 1), 1–2, 3–5, 7–8, 19–20, 22–23
Potter, Mary (see footnote, p. 1), 1, 2, 8, 9–11, 13
Potter, Sarah, (see footnote, p. 1), 8, 10–11, 13
Prevention Education Program, 92
"Primal scream" therapy, 173
"Projection", 160

Prostitutes and pimps, 86–87

Radical Reconstruction reformers, 66
Rank, Dee, 46–47
Rapists, serial, 141
Reality, child's, 34
Recanting allegations, xi, 16–17, 39–40, 50
Reese, Melvin Davis, 147–48
"Repetition compulsion", 157, 173
Report of the Committee on Sexual Offenses Against Children. *See* Badgley Report
Reporting of suspected abuse cases, 72–73, 75
Robie, Judge Ronald, 37
Roper pedophile study, 131
Rubin, Gail, 179–80
Rud, James, 42–43, 47–48, 50, 52–53, 127
Rundle, Christopher, 57
Rush, Florence, 79, 172–73

Sacramento case, 36–41
St. Jerome, 116
St. Vitus's Dance, 115
Salazar de Frias, Alonzo, 121–22
Salem witch trials, 122–26
Satanism, vii–ix, 11, 91, 107–29
Schreiber, Flora, 174
Serial murderers, xiii, 133–34, 137–39, 143–44
Serial rapists, 141
Sgroi–Giaretto treatment program, 94–95, 99
Sgroi, Suzanne, 32, 94–95, 96, 98, 99, 103–04
Silverman, F.N., 68–69
Socialization of children, 157–58
Society for the Prevention of Cruelty to Children (U.S.), 67
"Something About Amelia" (television movie), 45
Son of Sam (Berkowitz), 150
Spencer, Harriet, 162–63
Spree, Friedrich von, 121
Status of children as members of the state, 81–82
Steinlhauer, Dr. Paul, 22

Subcommittee on Government Information, Justice and Agriculture (1986, U.S.), 133–34
Sulzer, J., 171–72
Summit, Dr. Roland, 60, 91–92, child sexual abuse accommodation syndrome, 18, 27–29, 30–32, 40, 60, 79, 96–98
Sweden witch trials (1669), 123–24
Swenson study on sexual abuse, 132
Sybil (Flora Schreiber), 174

Tate, Sharon, 150
"Terrible Thing That Happened to Dolly, The" (Doris Bell), 37
Testimony of children, videotaping, 59–60, 88
Thou Shalt Not Be Aware (Alice Miller), 172
Tituba, 124–25
Trauma, community, 55
Treatment program. *See* Sgroi–Giaretto
Tucker, Gehl, 51

Underwager, Dr. Ralph, 33–35, 56, 61, 99, 103, 104, 132
United Nations' Declaration of the Rights of the Child, 67–68

Vancouver case, 104–05
Vermont case, x–xi
Victims of Child Abuse Laws (VOCAL), 33, 42, 98, 127
Videotaping children's testimony. *See* Testimony of children
Vincent, Dr. Charles, 122
Violent sexual offenders, 133–37

Wakefield, Bob, 88
Weininger, Dr. Otto, 110
Williams, Abigail, 124–25
Winters, E.F., 40
Witches, 114, 116–17
Witch-hunt, 107
Wyatt, Jane, 2, 8–15, 20–21, 25, 55

Zamora, Emil, 5
Zodiac killer, 148–50
Zundel, Ernst, 13